Set Free

A Miracle Remembered

Michael Gance

WestBow
PRESS
A DIVISION OF THOMAS NELSON

WestBow Press books may be ordered through booksellers or by contacting:

WestBow Press
A Division of Thomas Nelson
1663 Liberty Drive
Bloomington, IN 47403
www.westbowpress.com
1-(866) 928-1240

Because of the dynamic nature of the Internet, any web addresses or links contained in this book may have changed since publication and may no longer be valid. The views expressed in this work are solely those of the author and do not necessarily reflect the views of the publisher, and the publisher hereby disclaims any responsibility for them.

Any people depicted in stock imagery provided by Thinkstock are models, and such images are being used for illustrative purposes only.

Certain stock imagery © Thinkstock.

ISBN: 978-1-4497-6681-8 (e)
ISBN: 978-1-4497-6680-1 (sc)
ISBN: 978-1-4497-6682-5 (hc)

Library of Congress Control Number: 2012916633

Printed in the United States of America

WestBow Press rev. date: 11/21/2012

Contents

Acknowledgments:

I would like to thank my wife, Suzann, for her ever faithful support though the many challenging years of our life together. Being married to a drug addict is a very difficult challenge which takes a lot of character, commitment, and love of which she is a giant of an example.

I'd also like to thank my son Santino for choosing the right path in life by serving God, never making me feel guilty by following in the footsteps of a drug addict, and for always being respectful and courageous.

Lastly, I'd like to thank the late Pastor Ron Piedmonte. When others would have cast me away, he never gave up on me and always believed that I could change.

Introduction:

There is something about the presence of certain loved ones that enables the direction of our behavior to change effortlessly. If a man were to slam his finger with a hammer and his mother were standing right there next to him, he would be much less likely to swear. In the same way, there is nothing the nearness of Christ can't cure.

How are we empowered to be delivered from sin before we get into it? In His presence, as we abide in Him, and He in us, we will be naturally delivered before the event of our sin. In His presence is the power behind deliverance, and living there is the key. Teaching and understanding of the knowledge of Christ will not empower us. Only Christ's presence with us gives us power.

I love and respect Him, so I am delivered from my flesh – because He is with me, I slay the flesh easily – Christ in me is God's hope of ever getting anything out of me.

I

The Early Years

The story of a life often begins far before that life itself. My father, Tony Gance, met and married my mother, Lillian, in 1952 when he was twenty-seven. From my maternal grandparents' perspective, my mother had become involved with a man representing all that threatened their particular cultural identity and values. Fearful of this threat, they strongly disapproved of my father and eventually kicked my mother out of the house.

"Well, you're going to have to marry her now" concluded my paternal grandfather, even though my father had only been dating her for a short time. My grandfather was right in the sense that my mother had nowhere to go, having been abandoned by her family, marrying my father was really her only option. My father, not willing to shirk his responsibilities, took his father's advice and married my mother.

As I look back on my story, I cannot tell you if my father married my mother out of love, guilt, or perhaps a bit of both. I am, however, more able to speak from my father's perspective. My father had a strong sense of responsibility that was more than likely the driving force behind his actions and was undoubtedly rooted in his past. Our past forms us into the people we become, determining the choices we make.

My father was one of seven children. His mother had died shortly after giving birth to a set of twins. My grandfather, now the sole caretaker for five children and the new born twins, depended on my two aunts to shoulder much of the responsibility. In all this, my father learned at a young age that he was expected to do the right thing – to be a support to his family and to keep everything together. That pressure to keep things going, to react quickly and boldly before thinking, would be a pattern that continued in my father's life as his sense of responsibility became something more: a desire for control.

I was born five years into my parents' marriage. In my early years, I could feel the tension between my parents. Perhaps my father resented my mother's need to be rescued, or perhaps it was because they discovered too late how little they had in common. For whatever reason, they separated when I was three years old and were divorced by my seventh birthday. The painful length of the process had much to do with their association with the Catholic Church as well as the embarrassment they suffered after the ordeal was over which brought on a sense of shame that would cast a shadow into my own life.

In the wake of my parents' separation, I lived with my mother, who stopped at nothing to poison me against my father. She had so turned me against him that when he came to visit me when I was seven years old, I refused to have anything to do with him. This went on for three years.

Soon after the separation, my mother met a man named Bob Charlton at the Midway Bowling Alley where she began working and they quickly became romantically involved. Although I was only seven years old at the time, I had a bad feeling about their involvement. Much of my bad feeling had to do with my mother's habit of going to see Bob late at night. Sometimes she would bring me along with her. I would lay in the back seat covered by a blanket as my mother's blue Valiant rolled down the empty streets. I remember feeling the heat of my own breath beneath that blanket and the haunting tone of resignation in my mother's voice as she said to Bob, "You've made me do things I didn't want to do." I prayed that my mother would stop being with Bob, hoping that there was a way out of that blue Valiant and all it stood for – living a life with divorced parents. My prayers were answered soon thereafter when my mother broke things off with Bob.

When the divorce became final, my father acquired the house in the settlement, forcing my mother and me to relocate. We moved to Sidney, New York where I attended a new school. My mother's brother, Andy, lived in Sidney, and he and my mother reconnected. With my Uncle Andy's help, my mother got a job at the hotel he owned where he also offered us a place to live. It appeared things were looking up.

During this time, my mother began to develop a relationship with her second boyfriend, a man named Bob Murphy. While he proved to be an improvement over Bob Charlton, I still did not quite feel comfortable with their relationship. I disliked Bob almost from the start, just knowing inside myself that there was something wrong with the whole situation.

Six months after moving to Sidney, my mother and I moved again to Ithaca where Bob owned farmhouse and a gravel pit where my mother worked for him. I remember lying in my bed at night, fully aware of my mother sleeping in bed nearby with a man who was not my father. I felt more than uncomfortable, as though my mother and I were dirty. Despite my upbringing in a home full of tension and inconsistency, I had a strong sense of the way things should be, of how families ought to function. To complicate matters even further, Bob Murphy was not yet divorced from his first wife. Knowing this, I wondered if he ever planned on marrying my mother and making us a family. Deep within myself, I knew he had no such intention, especially since he already had five or six children with his wife. I knew then, at almost nine years of age, that whatever was going on in the master bedroom near me was wrong, that marriage promises should not be broken, and that families should stay together.

Looking back, I am amazed to see how God plants His truth and order into our hearts even before we come to know Him personally.

Moving to Ithaca meant that I had to change schools for a seventh time. As any child would, I found it difficult to adjust and find stability in a constantly changing environment. My mother had become very inconsistent, often leaving to go out with friends or Bob. When she was at home, she would drink occasionally. When Bob was home, she would sometimes drink for the whole night. Though I did not have much of a moral standard in my own life at the time, I knew that no good could come from my mother's drinking.

Beneath my discomfort at Bob's and my mother's lifestyle, the most intense feeling in my heart at the time was loneliness. We lived in a large house and my mother and Bob had their own room and I had mine. I felt as though I was a bother to them, as though I was being shut away and pushed to the side, far from the center of their lives. I would sit in my room at night, thinking about them drinking the night away in their bedroom on the other side of the house, and I felt so utterly alone. Again I prayed to God for a way out of my loneliness.

Again, I was heard.

My father, who I had been brainwashed into despising, got wind of my mother's situation – that she was becoming a heavy drinker and was living with a married man. He got a lawyer and came to Ithaca to claim his visitation rights with me.

When he came to get me, I had no idea what would happen or where I would stay. I had no choice. He just grabbed me, threw me over his shoulder, and locked me into the back of his car, insisting that he receive his visitation rights with his only son. He took me to his home in Endicott for the weekend. I was ten years old at that time.

My father owned a restaurant and he put me right to work washing dishes for the weekend. It was not exactly the kind of fun filled weekend that one might imagine for a ten-year-old boy, but at least I felt wanted, useful, and valued in some capacity. It was a better life than the one I had with my mother and Bob Murphy in Ithaca, where I felt invisible. This was when I started to consider that my mother might have been wrong about my father all along, that perhaps he wasn't such a bad guy after all.

My weekends in Endicott became a regular part of my life. My father would pick me up on Fridays after school, take me to work in the restaurant, and return me on Sunday nights before the start of a new week.

Meanwhile, all this made my mother very nervous. Perhaps she was afraid of losing me, despite how much she left me alone in the house anyway. One Friday afternoon, I returned home from school to find my mother sitting in the house with her sister, my aunt, Margaret. They started asking me what I had been doing, accusing me of telling my father all about my mother and Bob Murphy. I didn't even know what I could have said to make my mother so angry. I had not really said anything about her and Bob apart from what my father had already known. My aunt left the house after a while and then my mother left the house, not saying where she was going or when she would be back. I was ten years old, and it was dark outside and scary in that old farm house. So I called my dad.

"Mom left. I'm scared!" was all I managed to say. My father arrived to pick me up in less than forty-five minutes. We drove away from Bob Murphy's house that day, a place to which I would never again return.

I was glad to leave that house. I arrived at my father's with the hope of finding something more stable, some place where I could finally belong. My father had a wife, Judy, to whom he had been married for a little over two years when I came into their lives. Judy was young, only fourteen years older than me. I thought she was wonderful. She was young enough for me to think she was a lot of fun, but old enough to take it upon herself to care for me. She took pity on me, feeling I needed love and care. I was only ten years old, but I was overweight and had terribly crooked teeth. Judy and my father arranged for me to have braces to straighten out my teeth. Judy was warm and affectionate toward me and I felt like I was finally home. After a while I was comfortable enough to call her "mom."

The first Thanksgiving that I spent with my father and Judy, a relative came to stay with us. We stayed in the same room because we only had two bedrooms at the time. I awoke in the middle of the night with the feeling that someone was touching me. I was too young to really understand anything more than something was happening to me that shouldn't have been. I decided to keep quiet about what had happened, but when I heard that this relative was coming over again for Christmas I decided to tell my father. I had not told anyone up until that point because I was afraid. When I told my father I knew that he was supposed to do something to protect me, but he did nothing. He chose to ignore me in a moment when I desperately needed him to hear me and to rescue me. This made me feel terrible and unloved. It also made me feel as though I wasn't worth standing up for.

Christmas came and went without alarm. The abuse never happened again, but the memory of it stayed with me for years as did the thought that there was no one who would be there to keep me safe and stand up for what was best for me. I was ten years old, living with my father and stepmother, but I had no one in my corner, no allies. I still had not found where I belonged or where I could be loved. I had not found my home. It was this feeling of vulnerability, isolation, and the idea of not being worthy enough to be protected, that had set me up for what was to come in my life.

As the years went by, the symptoms of my pain and loneliness would motivate me to find ways to cope with rather than address the deep needs in my heart. I preferred to look for temporary relief rather than begin the messy and painful process of healing from these events.

On the outside I was able to live a relatively normal life. I got along well with Judy because she was very good to me. I was working in my father's restaurant and feeling good about myself as a result, but I still felt like an outsider in my own home. I began smoking cigarettes when I was thirteen. This didn't matter to my father or stepmother as long as I did so in my room where no one could see me. My parents would remind me that our "family" was in a public business – my father owned a restaurant and it was important to maintain a certain appearance. In my family appearance was valued far above reality.

As I lifted a cigarette to my lips, always in my room, I quietly came to the conclusion that I could be one person inside my house and another outside of it. This idea didn't sit well inside me as my deep sense of morality and the way things should be came into conflict with the reality of my present life, just as it had several times before. I didn't realize it at the time but my discomfort stemmed from something I would come to know as hypocrisy. It was no longer the hypocrisy of my mother, father, or even Bob Murphy; it was mine that was causing my stomach to turn with a sense of guilt and dirtiness.

I started to feel that I could do whatever I wanted when no one was looking. I could be a different person by myself than I was in public. I began to see that I could have two selves – my public, professional self, and my private self. The person who worked in my father's restaurant all day and the boy who smoked cigarettes behind closed doors were the same person, but I could close my eyes and pretend that they were not. Furthermore, no one cared enough to discipline me, to call me out on my hypocrisy, and encourage me to reconcile my two selves. No one did this and so the chasm grew larger, hypocrisy became more and more accepted in my life, and in the years following, it became my life.

Isolation was still very much a problem in my life; it had been when I lived with my mother and Bob. I was living in a beautiful, expensively decorated house with my father and stepmother Judy. The house was large enough for me to have my own wing, which included a bathroom, bedroom, and small living room just for me. Despite all of the material things I enjoyed, I still felt as though my father, Judy, and I were not a complete family. Whenever we would go on vacations I was always allowed – encouraged even – to bring along a friend. On one hand this was wonderful for me because it gave me the chance to play with someone my own age. At the same time, I would consider the friend I had brought along with me and couldn't help but wonder if my father and Judy didn't want anything to do with me, if they just didn't want me to bother them. They were entertaining me all the while securing privacy for themselves, time for them to spend together. That, I thought, was not a family.

In this way life with my father and Judy, though largely peaceful and normal, was not what it should have been. Years later – when I realized God's true plan for marriages and families – I saw that I had been fed a bad value system from the very beginning. I was taught that working was all that mattered, and money was all that mattered. My father had made a great deal of money, married a woman much younger than he, and defined success on those narrow terms. Not only did he value his success, he worshipped it. I began to kneel to the same god as I grew older and spent more and more time working at the restaurant.

There was no sort of moral foundation in our home, no sense that what we did when we were by ourselves mattered or affected who we were. There was no sense that money was a tool to be used to help others and to provide for a family. Money was the objective, the goal of all hard work. We didn't have each other as a source of unconditional love and support. What we did have were our shiny lives, all aglow with our successes, dazzling, without an ounce of substance below the surface. We had our money, our house, and our business. Our stomachs were full while our souls were starving to death, and we didn't even realize it. I knew inside myself that there had to be more than this endless pursuit of something as elusive as success.

When I was fourteen years old, my father suffered his first heart attack. As he recovered, he swore off smoking and began walking for exercise. After his heart attack, my father began to collect social security. At this time, he told me that he was planning to someday give me the restaurant. Of course I was thrilled; I had been working in that restaurant for about four years now and had come to enjoy the food business. I saw myself possibly running a restaurant one day. At the age of fourteen, I worked in the restaurant every night after school. I learned a variety of new skills, and I enjoyed every minute of it.

When I was sixteen I got my driver's license and the little bit of extra independence that came with it. At this time, the high school I was attending was under construction, making many classrooms unavailable for use during the course of the school day. To accommodate these changes, the school had half of the students come in the morning and the other half come in the evening. I would go to school during the morning hours, then go to work in the restaurant in the afternoon. As I approached graduation, I found out that I was not going to graduate because I had not been going to my gym classes. This did not bother me too much; I was involved in the restaurant and had the promise of one day owning it myself.

Despite the promise of this future, I felt unaccomplished for not finishing high school. It seemed like an important thing to do. I had always felt the pressure to measure up and succeed, mostly from my own father. But, as had become my habit, I kept pursuing the temporary sense of fulfillment that came from earning money and – for a little while – I forgot all about being lonely. Soon I would learn that the means by which I would forget my emptiness would only grow darker and darker.

II

The Darkness Begins

When I was eighteen, I had not graduated from high school, and I was working in my father's restaurant full-time. Even though this was not the normal life of a teenager, I had carved out a sort of community for myself from among the other workers at the restaurant. I had settled into the routine of working as much as I could while trying to enjoy what little leisure time I had.

There was a man who lived in the apartment above my father's restaurant by the name of Phil. Phil married a woman named Marilyn from New York City. Marilyn had a brother named Mike who would come up on weekends to visit. Marilyn asked me to show Mike around while he was in town and I agreed. Mike was friendly and outgoing and we became best friends. I looked forward to the weekends when

Mike would come to town and we would go out drinking after work was over. Eventually, Mike moved to the area from New York City and we began to go out every single night.

For the next three years I fell into a pattern: Mike and I would work all day, and then spend our free time at night going from bar to bar until early the next morning. All this was happening around the rise of disco, platform shoes, and hair permanents, and we were in the middle of it.

Materialism and externalism were all that mattered during these exhilarating days of my youth. I was wearing the best, most expensive, clothes and doing everything to appear as though I was worth a million dollars. On the inside there was still a longing to really be worth something and the fear that I wasn't worth anything at all. But I drowned my insecurities and worries in alcohol, with the noise of nightclubs, and in the endless daily grind of working at the restaurant. I did not allow myself time to feel the depth of my emptiness or the fullness of my longing. Mike and I had discovered a world that we never knew existed or was available, but I was ready for it. I was ready for a world that made me feel good, forget my pain, and that revolved around me. I was ready for a world that centered around my feeling good and where there were no consequences.

There was alcohol, there were women, and there was an energy that could make me forget anything I didn't have. I realized that I could drink away my loneliness, the lingering feeling that I didn't belong in my own home, and my deep fear that I didn't matter. Like everyone else around me, I bought into the idea that how I looked was all that mattered, and that my worth was measured by how much money I could make. It was a superficial time, and I was knee-deep in all the glitz and glamour – without an ounce of substance. It was an enchanted, flashy world, where it was always tonight, always now, and never tomorrow. Deep inside, I knew none of it was real, but that didn't stop me from pretending.

It was there, in the middle of all the drinking and partying, that I had my first exposure to cocaine. The drug was rising in popularity at the time and, since we were on the cusp of all that was new and exciting, it was easily accessible to us. As I watched my friends pass cocaine around I felt uncertain about it, and I was wary of trying it. Despite the noise around me, something was holding me back; it was the whisper of my conscience. It was not quite fear, but perhaps the sense that it was just not right.

Even with all the night clubbing and drinking, I never really did any drugs. I would hear the stories of heroin addicts and pot smokers, and I wanted nothing to do with that. I was cool; I had money and style – or so I thought. Even so, after almost a year of not going along with a crowd of friends who were using cocaine, I went to an afterhours party at my friend Frank's apartment where everyone was using cocaine. I tried to subtly miss my turn whenever it came my way, avoiding it by excusing myself to the bathroom. I began to watch my friends at the party to see what effects this new drug had. They all appeared to be fine, and I began to wonder what the possible harm could be. I finally tried it, and the first time I really didn't feel anything at all. It was almost a letdown. What did happen, however, was that I really was no longer afraid of the mysterious new substance; I had broken down some of my inhibitions.

Wanting to feel something, I began to try cocaine more and more, until it began to bring with it a strange euphoria and an excitement that was both exhilarating and reassuring at the same time. Under its spell I found I had no worries, no loneliness, and no pain. Eventually, cocaine became a part of our lives. It just became another thing Mike and I did. It was another thing that helped us forget our troubles. It was another way for me to inject good feelings into myself, even if they weren't real and even if they would fade with time. It was good enough.

Everyone has some way that they escape the present and the monotony of their lives. Some eat, some drink, some have their relationships. I had cocaine, and I began to escape with it whenever I could and even when I couldn't. Soon cocaine was not just a weekend activity. It began to bleed into my weeknights and affect my work at the restaurant. By now I was spending a great deal of money to support my new found habit. To supplement some of this cost I began selling cocaine myself. This became especially dangerous.

Years before when my father went into the restaurant business he was told, "You can either drink alcohol or sell it when you own a bar, but you can't do both." Well, this principle also applies to drugs. You can't be a drug addict and sell drugs. Eventually it overtakes you, you can't function, and you lose everything. The advice was wise and behind it was the principle that control needed to be maintained at all times, there had to be boundaries, limits. But before long, I had abandoned these words and the wisdom behind them, forsaking limits and boundaries, and in the end, losing control of my life altogether. I lost control because I had given myself over to an addiction and to the feeding of that addiction, no matter what the cost.

It was not just my dad I was trying to avoid when I resorted to cocaine, I was also looking for a way to relieve the pressures of life and the burden of responsibility that was growing heavier and heavier on my shoulders. A few years before when my father had suffered his heart attack, it was not enough to incapacitate him, but it was enough to put him on disability and exempt him from running the restaurant.

A few years later, my father signed the restaurant over to me instead of selling it and he kept working his regular hours. The only thing that had changed was that the restaurant was in my name, and at first, this was of little difference to me. As time went on, however, I began to feel a sense of ambition growing inside of me and gaining momentum.

I had been working long hours at the restaurant for a few years now; I was motivated by my desire to be successful and to make more money. Though I had been working a lot my arrangement with my father was that he still received 75% of the restaurant's gross profits while I got the other 25%. As we became more successful through the years, this became a great deal of money to me. I wanted to expand and open more restaurants but my father didn't. Although my father had signed the restaurant over to me, he did not cease to control its operation; I was still subordinate to him. I became aware of the limits that surrounded me, and subconsciously, began to resent them.

Looking back I suspect that my promise and talent made my father nervous. At a young age I demonstrated an inclination for business, I had vision and motivation, and I was smart and efficient. I had big dreams for the restaurant too, but my father was not following my lead. When I was nineteen years old, I saw an opportunity to buy a second restaurant with a man named Bob Granger. My father, though he was successful, operated largely in fear. He was always wary of changes and new ideas, and thus my tendency to be a visionary threatened him and his desire to be safe, to stay with what worked. My father went along with the Bob Granger deal until he realized, with the way I put it together, the plan would work and the deal would go through.

When my father realized the deal would work it made him very nervous and he started to pull back. He put so many constraints on us that the deal finally did fall through. I was deeply disappointed, and I took my father's actions personally, as though he was attacking me, my dreams, and my visions. When it came to my father, I was always running ahead, and yet, he always seemed to be holding me back. My promise and potential as a restaurant owner not only threatened my father, but it also put a great deal of pressure on me. My father and I were similar in this way; we both had fears that created more obstacles for our success than any other outside factors could have. Although I was more willing to take risks than he, I too lived in fear of failure. When this fear became overwhelming, I turned to cocaine as a means of escape, trying to find a place where I was not under tremendous pressure.

Now that I am a father, I see that my father did me a disservice by giving me so much responsibility at such a young age. He didn't know when to protect me and when to challenge me. He allowed me to earn large amounts of money rather than increasing my responsibilities and compensation as I matured. This sent me speeding into an adult world when I was still very much a youth, too young and easily overwhelmed to be a real adult. This created the conflict I felt inside between the responsibility I had to my father and the responsibility I felt I had to my own talent and desire to see where my ideas could go. I was frustrated that while my father gave me so much of the restaurant's profit, I had little control over the business itself. I could not realize the dreams I had for the restaurant, and in my desire for control, and frustration for lack of it, I found a counterfeit solace in cocaine – where I felt nothing. No frustration, no desires, just nothing at all.

I was using every day and after a few years I began to feel the effects of my cocaine habit more and more, especially the mental ones. Incessant cocaine use often carries with it a tendency toward paranoia. I remember working in the restaurant and looking up to see cars parked outside. Fears inside me began to unfold, as I became certain that the FBI had come for me. I began to lose all sense of security and safety, as if I were always being watched by someone, as if danger were constantly imminent, and I could not escape it; I could not find a safe place. My desire for escape had pushed me deeper and deeper into cocaine use and deeper into an unforgiving darkness.

Despite the chaotic state of my inner life, I managed to maintain a semblance of normalcy on the outside. I kept working hard at the restaurant and going out with Mike Tortora every night like clockwork. Though I lacked the most essential disciplines, my life had a rhythm and a sense of predictability on which I could depend. This rhythm, however, would not last forever. Mike Tortora decided to get married and though I knew things would not be exactly the same, I did not foresee what this change would do to me inside. Mike had been working with his brother-in-law, Phil since he had arrived in Binghamton a few years prior. Phil and Mike's sister Marilyn had made plans to buy another business in Florida, where they planned to someday retire. Mike had no real plans for his future in Binghamton, so this was a good opportunity for him. Soon after his wedding, he and his new wife moved down to Florida and out of my life. As I stood up in Mike's wedding, I had no idea how deeply I would be affected by the loss of my best friend. One day, we were together laughing and drinking, and the next Mike was gone and I was all alone.

The feelings of loneliness and worthlessness, that had haunted me since my childhood, were beginning to rise to the surface of my life once again. I quickly buried them with cocaine, which I used even more in Mike's absence. It was one of the lowest spots in my life up to that point and I had no idea how much lower I would have to go before finally beginning some sort of ascent to a real, meaningful life. By this time, my father had discovered my cocaine use, which only added more of a strain to our relationship.

Somewhere inside me, I still heard the whisper of my conscience. I knew that my cocaine habit was wrong. I was not making a good choice though I was not sure why. Looking back, I see that even when I was young, I had a sense of morality, a sense of what I should and should not have been doing. But it was not anchored; I didn't understand what God wanted from me or how I had need of Him. My religious experience to date had not given any kind of moral foundation – it had just been another place in my life where I saw hypocrisy.

When I was in eighth grade, I had to have my appendix removed. At that time an appendectomy kept someone my age in the hospital for a week. In the wake of this event, I was able to have time off from the restaurant for the weekend. One of those nights, there was a dance at my school for the ninth graders. I had many friends in ninth grade, and so I made my way to the school to meet up with them. I was stopped by a priest who reminded me, less than gently, that I was not to be there because I was not in ninth grade. Not seeing why this was such an issue, I continued to talk with my friends. The priest came back and threw me up against a wall, telling me to leave. I felt instant pain in the stitches I had, fresh from my recent surgery. "I just had my appendix removed," I gasped to the priest. Then, with anger setting in I said, "I'll see that my father sends you the bill."

It also never sat well with me that Judy was not allowed to take communion since she had married a divorced man. I saw no place in the church for myself, no place to be accepted, or to receive any kind of balm for my loneliness and insecurities. I, like so many others, made no differentiation between God and the people of the church. I felt rejected by the church and, consequently, felt rejected by God as well. I believed in God, to be sure, but I saw Him as the embodiment of all that was good and right, all that was supposed to be. I knew the way the priest had treated me was neither good nor right, and this only added to my perception that the church and my idea of God had little to do with one another. The church was more a place of problems than solutions.

Overall, I was seeing in the church what I was seeing in so many aspects of my own life: reality was so far from ideal, things were not as they ought to be, and the response always seemed to be to pretend that they were.

Pretending that everything was alright and settling for the semblance of peace and security without the substance of it: these were the practices that had prepared me for cocaine. As I look back, my life had been preparing me all along. I had an appearance of security with my mother, the semblance of family with my father and Judy, and eventually a form of fulfillment in working for my father. The substance of these things – security, family, and fulfillment – could not have been farther from my reach. What was within my reach was cocaine along with the emptiness it never failed to deliver.

III

Sue

Mike Tortora's departure left me feeling more alone than I had ever felt before, and I made sordid attempts to remedy that loneliness with more cocaine, more women, and more distractions. But I was beginning to learn that life could not continue at such a pace, that eventually, the effects if cocaine would wear off. Women would come and go out of my life. I began to realize that I did not even care, not one of these women really mattered to me, or so I thought. One night soon after New Year's Eve of 1979, I was out with my parents and a date at a bar called Beau Jon's. In the midst of the noise and activity of the club I saw, who I quickly believed to be the most beautiful girl I had ever laid eyes on, sitting right there at the bar.

I remembered Suzann from high school years ago and, as I looked at her, I hoped with all possible sincerity that she remembered me too. I was fortunate that night because Suzann recognized me and waved me over to where she was sitting. I quickly began to try to think of a way to get rid of the date I had brought with me. Most of the crowd from Beau Jon's went over to Dino's. I had one of my friends dance with Kathy, my date, while giving me the chance to talk to Sue at the bar. Wishing to spend more time with Sue, I realized I would have to get rid of Kathy for the evening. I finally told her I was sick and would regretfully have to bring her home. On my way out with Kathy, I made sure to ask Sue to meet me at the restaurant later for an afterhours party. I unloaded Kathy and excitedly made my way to the restaurant. Sue never showed up.

I was disappointed, but decided to be persistent. I called Sue the next day to see where she had been. Her sister Bonnie was the one to answer the phone. Sue, who had not been impressed with me the night before, did not want to talk to me. After several attempts at charm, I was able to get her on the phone, and after another many tries I finally convinced her to go on a date with me.

I battled natural first date nerves as I drove to pick her up. I didn't realize then, dressed in my finest, that the woman coming into my life that night would bring more than I had anticipated. Had I known where my relationship with Sue would one day lead and how it would change me, I wonder if I would have walked into that house like I did that night with a bottle of wine in hand to impress Sue's mother.

Since I had known Sue in high school, she had moved to Las Vegas to work as a cocktail waitress and then to Lake Tahoe to work with her brother-in-law in a casino dealing poker. Knowing this, I assumed she would share my affinity for cocaine, and I took her back to my apartment where I had some for her to try before we went to dinner. "I don't do that stuff," she replied when I showed her what I had. Surprised, and a little unsure of how to respond, I just took Sue to dinner. I had always known my cocaine usage was wrong but, until then, it didn't seem to matter. My father didn't know how bad it was, it didn't affect my work at the restaurant, and all of my friends used with me. I would often think to myself that no one cared. There were no boundaries; there never were any, not until that moment when Sue told me she "didn't do that stuff," the moment, the short moment, when I wished I didn't either.

I saw Sue a few more times during the holiday as the time neared for her to return to her job. I asked her to consider staying in Binghamton with me, as I had begun to care for her, and I didn't want our time together to come to an end. Sue wasn't sure she wanted to return after all. She had spent several years drinking and living a wild lifestyle in Las Vegas and then Lake Tahoe. Years later, she told me that as she looked out the window of her airplane on the eastward flight from Lake Tahoe, she told God that if He would give her a husband and a real, fulfilling life, she would not return to Lake Tahoe, and that she would serve Him. She didn't know sitting there in that airplane that God would hold up His end of that deal, nor did she know how long and winding the road would be to its fulfillment, or how He would bring her there. To my delight, Sue stayed in town and did not return to Lake Tahoe.

Spring came and by the summer time Sue and I saw each other just about every day. My father and Judy had a cottage where Sue and I would spend my days off and have fun together. The summer went by and it was autumn before I knew it. I remember the day in November when Sue told me she was pregnant. I was working in the restaurant when she stopped by unexpectedly.

"I need to talk to you" she said. Her voice was flat. I looked up for a moment before nodding for her to continue on.

"I just found out I'm pregnant," she crossed her arms over her chest, not angry, just hugging herself. Her eyes were full of questions – for which I knew I had no answers. The answer I decided on was probably not the best one.

"You don't have to keep it." The words came out fast, too fast for me to stop them but fast enough for me to regret them. I didn't know what to do. I tried to redeem myself,

"Thursday is my day off. Can we talk about it on Thursday?" It was Monday. I knew I had done little to offer any comfort or security to Sue. The truth was that I had little of those things to offer. Was I even ready to be a father?

When Thursday came I kept face. I told Sue that we would probably get married. We had mentioned it in the past few months. I loved Sue, and I knew that I wanted to be with her, but something inside me still felt the sharp sensations of fear when I considered marrying her and meeting my child in a matter of months. I was daunted by the permanence of marriage. All my life I had desired stability and a real home where I belonged; but then, contemplating marriage to a beautiful woman, I found myself afraid of the very thing I wanted in my heart. Perhaps deep inside I didn't think I deserved it. Perhaps I knew I didn't. Marriage was not only permanent, it was intimate. It was a place where I would have to be known by Sue. I would have to go home to her every night and in this, risk exposure of Sue discovering the hold that cocaine had on my life. I was afraid of this woman realizing the seriousness of my addiction, the depth of my darkness.

For so many years I had been alone, worrying only for myself and damaging only myself. Soon I would have a wife and child. Naturally, I turned to cocaine to relieve my fears and tensions even though it was my addiction to cocaine and my fear of discovery that was truly fueling my fear of marrying Sue. Cocaine, as it had been in the past, was once again both my vice and my escape. I thought I was finding relief in cocaine, a way out, when really I was only falling deeper into darkness with every use.

Our engagement was announced around Christmas, almost a year to the day we saw each other at Beau Jon's. Sue's mother had a party for us, and it was here that I was to present Sue with her engagement ring. In the grip of my fear, I went only halfway on the ring. Rather than the engagement ring I was expected to buy her, I got a cocktail ring. It was something that didn't feel so serious, so permanent. Deep inside I knew I should have made a different choice.

In front of Sue's family, I opened the ring box and held out the cocktail ring to her, the woman I loved and desperately wanted to love more. My instinct was confirmed when a humiliated Sue burst into tears. She knew what she deserved, and she knew that the ring in my hands was certainly not it.

I looked down at the cocktail ring as it glistened in the light; it was beautiful to behold, but it was not the symbol of commitment it was supposed to be. I knew inside myself that I was just like that cocktail ring; not good enough, not what I should have been, and a cheap semblance of security and commitment. I loved Sue, but I was afraid of all that the future had in store. I knew that in my heart I didn't trust her, because I knew in my heart that she had no reason to trust me.

Despite my blunder with the ring, Sue did decide to stay with me, following her heart. When she moved back to Binghamton permanently, Sue began working at The Owego Treadway as a cocktail waitress. She made some friends there and would often go out with those girls. On the nights that they went out my cocaine-induced paranoia would take control of me. I would sometimes drive up to the Owego Treadway in my pajamas to spy on Sue, so convinced that my delusions of her having another boyfriend were true. Beneath these delusions was the real fear that I was just undeserving of love. My father had never offered me the love and acceptance I wanted and my stepmother Judy had her own life to deal with. My biological mother had abandoned me in the innocence of my childhood; why wouldn't Sue abandon me as well? Once she inevitably learned what I really was, and of the dark addiction that controlled my life, what possible reason would she have to remain faithful to me?

My father was less than supportive of my impending marriage to Sue. It was his pattern to dislike the girls I dated if I took them out more than a few times. He didn't want me to be distracted from my work at the restaurant. It was hard to take women on dates when I was always expected to work during the peak hours of the evening. For my father, work and the restaurant always came before anything else: family, relationships, or even money. I thought for a long time that he was motivated by the potential of wealth, but really, underneath it all, work wasn't about money, it was about success, self approval, and adequacy.

Addictions are like that, whether it is cocaine, alcohol, or even work. Achieving success can be a strong motivator, and once it is achieved, maintaining it becomes the new focus. Working hard and long becomes all you know after a while

– the only thing that makes sense. Eventually, money stops being important. The end doesn't matter because the means have become therapeutic; the pattern becomes something that traps you in. That's addiction: an endless repetition of an action that you cannot stop because, deep inside, you do not know who you are without it, and you are too afraid to find out. My father couldn't bring himself face to face with who he might be without the restaurant any more than I could pry myself away from cocaine. We were both trapped.

I remember asking my father to close the restaurant on a Saturday for my wedding. He refused, forcing Sue and I to marry on a Sunday instead. Being forced to get married on a Sunday was deeply hurtful to Sue. It was just another way in which my father showed his sorely misplaced priorities. His restaurant, success, and money were much more important than family. Our wedding was not worth missing one day of business. Giving in, Sue and I agreed to wed on Sunday so that my father would grace us with his presence. Even after all that, on the Friday night before our wedding, Sue and I were driving up from the church to the rehearsal dinner when we were greeted by the lights and sounds of an ambulance outside of Gance's. My father was having an angina attack due to stress, for which my aunts blamed me. Looking back, they were right in a way. My father, though he did not know the specifics of my drug problem, knew that I was out of control, and our lives had been parallel for so long – not to mention that I held an important role in his business – that he was nervous over the uncertainty of my life. Everything he had invested in me, everything with which he had trusted me and built with me over the years was at risk of falling apart and he knew it.

Besides blaming Sue's and my marriage for my father's compromised health, my aunts did not hold Sue in high regard. Like most people would at the time, they had their own ideas of what it meant to live in Las Vegas, and they assumed her to be a wild woman. They saw her as just another person that would continue to enable me in my own wild lifestyle. As far as they could see, Sue was not a step in the right direction. My family, so concerned with appearances and how things looked from the outside, never thought that there was something else beneath the surface. My father, with all his money and success, rarely showed any kind of character. Meanwhile, I was the biggest loser of them all with my dark secret. Then there was Sue who was trying to leave her wild lifestyle behind and find some sense of stability and goodness with me. That was the truth, the real story. But when judgments are made solely on appearances with no thought to what lies beneath, the real story is seldom heard or understood.

Sue and I did marry despite the complications that had arisen along the way. We went on our honeymoon, first to Hawaii and then to Lake Tahoe to visit Sue's sister. It was there in Lake Tahoe that Sue began to notice the extent of my drinking and drug use. Until then, my time with her had been planned, not constant as it was on our honeymoon. This was what I had been afraid of all along; of Sue finding out how bad I was, of seeing me in a different light, and possibly rejecting me. But Sue did not reject me. Instead, she turned a blind eye to the drinking, just as she had to the drugs before. I was relieved, thinking that I was safe.

Later, I would learn the value of exposure and that love doesn't turn a blind eye, but brings problems and struggles to the light. But that was a long time from happening. We returned from our honeymoon and tried to settle into married life. In the days before our marriage, I would go out every night after work, drink, and do cocaine. Now I had a pregnant wife waiting for me at home which meant that my cocaine use became intensely private and more frequent. I was beginning to use all the time and at different times of the day, but always in secret.

IV

Trying to Cover My Tracks

Since everyone I knew drank heavily, it was easy to mask my addiction. Yet at the same time, Sue's suspicions were growing. She noticed I consumed a large amount of alcohol; more than what was socially acceptable, even for heavy drinkers. Before I was married, I would go out and drink and party all night long after I was done working at the restaurant. I was accustomed to drinking at large. When I got married and felt obliged to stay home with my wife, I still felt the urge to maintain my alcohol addiction. I would drink more and more at home rather than go out to get drunk. My nightly ritual was no longer in place. When I failed to limit my drinking and cocaine consumption to the nighttime after work hours, I found myself taking in more alcohol and cocaine throughout the day.

Addiction tightens its grip when whatever poison you feed yourself is not limited to ritual. It begins to bleed in, consuming the free moments of your day, then the moments that belong to something else until all of them, every waking moment, is in some way consumed and controlled by that addiction.

Sue and I were living in an apartment building that I had bought before we got married with the intention of renovating it and renting it out in order to pay the mortgage. It was a sensible investment for me to make, until I started dipping into the money I had set aside to do the remodeling. I tried to keep Sue from finding out about the problem, or at least from discovering its severity. Externally, everything was going well for me. I was successful at work, and had a beautiful wife and child on the way. But inside nothing was right, and inside, I knew it. That chasm that had been running between the calm appearance I maintained on the outside and the chaotic darkness of my private world was growing larger. Soon that darkness would have to come into the light and my dipping into our rent and remodeling profits put me on the road to exposure.

Eventually the money ran out, and I had to tell Sue, and my father-in-law, that we didn't have the funds to finish the apartment house. It was not the first time my drug use had been discovered, but it was the first time that it had been so costly to anyone other than me. Now I had a wife, a child, and a father-in-law who was helping us remodel the apartment. There were people depending on me; I was no longer just hurting myself with my addiction, and I did not bear the consequences alone. Finally, I had to tell my wife the truth about the money. I was a fool to think that she did not have her suspicions. She never thought that I had an addiction severe enough to eat up so much of our money and so much of our lives. I remember how she fainted to the floor when I finally told her. Later, Sue told me that in that moment she did not just faint in horror of my addiction and the realization that I had been living a lie; she fainted as she realized that then, more than ever before, she was under my father's control and that we were all at his mercy. He would have to give us money to finish the apartment house, and now we would have to fully depend on him, and my working for him, to support ourselves. Sue's feelings towards my father were less than congenial, especially since our wedding. From the beginning of our marriage, she saw how he controlled me and how he put pressure on me at the restaurant. It terrified her to feel his grip on our lives tighten in the event of our financial troubles.

Though Sue has seen from the beginning how unhealthy my relationship with my father was, she did not know what to do. She noticed how he exerted control over me that did not allow me to really be myself or do anything for myself. Sue felt trapped, especially when she realized how bad my addiction was. When she found out about how I had really spent the remodeling money, she got a glimpse into the reality that the thing which held an even tighter grip on us than my father was my addiction to cocaine.

The remodeling of our apartment should have cost us about $60,000, $20,000 of which I spent through to buy cocaine. Letting down Sue and her father was humiliating, but things became even worse when more and more people found out about my cocaine addiction. When my friend Mike Tortora had left town I was so miserable and I had been borrowing money from a bank under the guise of remodeling the restaurant. As word of my drug addiction got out, the bank caught wind of what I had really been doing with the money. My father found out and overnight, I went from being hailed as a boy genius restaurant manager to an incompetent drug addict. My reputation was destroyed. My father arranged for me to have some rehabilitation counseling with a man named Ron Gatano, and he also took the restaurant back; it was no longer in my name. I was limited to working in the kitchen on a modest salary. I had never fallen so low before. I had never gotten in so deep that I couldn't dig myself out. Humiliated and having lost everything, I ceased my cocaine use for a little while.

Despite the strength of its hold on me, cocaine was not an ever present demon in my life. When things were going badly, as they were at this point, I found that I was able to keep myself from using it. This was mostly due to the fact that I did not have sufficient funds to support my habit. But it was more than that, I knew how to deal with crisis when it came my way, I was able to take things into my own hands when they were going badly and do my best to make things right. I learned this from my childhood. But, as always, it was when things were already going well that my problem would flair up again. The darkness of cocaine would re-enter and take over, eventually pulling me back down into another period of crisis. My addiction spiraled out of control during high points in my life, not low ones, always sabotaging my success rather than exacerbating my failures. Cocaine had the chance to do this because inside, I did not feel worthy of anything I had; success, family, or even real love. My own insecurities and self-loathing swung the door open for cocaine to come and wreak havoc in my life. That way, disaster and heartbreak were at least my fault. So if I could not have success, family, or real love, I could have one thing: control.

In the midst of my exposure and humiliation, I did my best to get back on my feet. Prior to this failure, I had been thinking of ways to establish independence from my father. I was bright and young with many ideas for the business, and I wasn't sure if he was supportive of my desire to make those ideas reality. One of my best ideas at the time was to get a kitchen where we could process food, especially chicken, and sell this processed food to distribution lines such as Maine's and SYSCO Food Companies.

Since my responsibilities at the restaurant had changed, and I was itching to get out from under my father's control, I went ahead with my idea for the chicken processing plant. I found a federal kitchen I could rent from the Alamo Restaurant, and I was able to start up the business. First we began by selling chicken cutlets, and the idea took right off. I realized that I was going to need more space for the business. I talked to my father, who had purchased a gas station years before, and put it in my name. Since it was near the restaurant, he used it as an overflow parking lot, but did nothing with the actual building. I thought it would be a perfect place to move the manufacturing plant that had already grown quite successful.

My recent achievements with my new business had gone a little way to restoring my father's faith in me, so he agreed to help me remodel the gas station. I took out a building loan to remake it into a chicken processing plant, and kept on with my business, which I had decided to call Gance's Gourmet Foods. In addition to chicken cutlets, we began to sell chicken cordon bleu, chicken Kiev, and stuffed chicken breasts. My new products had found a buyers' market in places like Maine's, SYSCO companies, Giant, ShopRite, and Casa Imports, and many other companies wanted to work with us too. It seemed that things were looking up. Success on my own was within reach.

The business began to grow as I hired more people and solicited customers during the day while still working at the restaurant in the evenings. It was a difficult life, working day and night and barely having any time at home. This routine began to take its toll on me. I felt as though I was running myself ragged trying to keep everyone in my life happy. The stress of my present situation opened the door for cocaine to once again come in and take control.

V

On the Rebound

These moments when things would look up, when success was in reach, were defining moments for me. It was as though I was running on some sort of adrenaline, everything was clear and I was able to make good decisions that made me successful. But then, something would happen; with everything going right I would feel inside me a sickening sense of fear, as though I was under pressure, as if any day now, it was all going to end. I knew of only one way to cope with fears, and that was when the door for cocaine swung open again, and the darkness began to re-invade my life. It was as though deep inside me, I didn't want to succeed; I couldn't bear to be successful. I began spending the profit from Gance's Gourmet Foods on cocaine, and within a year, I had eaten though so much money that I knew I had two options: either find cash to keep the business afloat, or find some way out of the business altogether.

As it did with the apartment house, my struggle with cocaine brought its share of financial troubles to my new enterprise. I had a loyal customer named Jerry Goldman who was in the production business, making sandwiches for vending machines. He believed in what I was doing and so I invited him into partnership with me. I thought that if I could invite someone else into what I knew would eventually be a failure due to my inability to succeed, then I would not be alone in this failure, or even that I might have a scapegoat. With my addiction constantly looming over me, I was growing desperate in every conceivable way.

Together Jerry and I were able to make the business a corporation and my plan was for the new corporation to pay enough rent for me to be able to pay off my debts that I had built up with my repeated cocaine use. Jerry and I had a good understanding of each other when he came in with me, but I think he saw right away that I had problems and that I wasn't able to manage myself.

When a person's drug use becomes full time, as did my own, keeping the addiction hidden starts to take up more time and energy. Sue thought that I had ceased my cocaine use since the apartment remodeling fiasco a few months before. She did not know how my vulnerability to cocaine increased with the rate of my success, which to me equated the possibility of failure. Hiding my addiction from Sue, my father, and now Jerry, proved to be too much for me, and I began to neglect my responsibilities at the chicken plant. Jerry, taking notice of my negligence, became unwilling to pay the rent on which I depended to keep the plant open.

"You can't do your job, Mike" I remember him saying the day he left. "You come in late all the time, you don't hold up your end of things."

"Jerry, I don't know what to tell you" I would mutter, although I knew exactly what I should tell him. I knew exactly why things were going the way they were going. It was me who kept us down. It was cocaine, but really, it was me.

"Are you saying you want out?" I feared Jerry's answer, as it would mean that I was, again, alone in my failure.

"That's what I'm saying, Mike, even though I think this could be a good thing, but right now, there's something wrong, Mike, with all of this, with you." Jerry had no idea the depth to which he was right. But I certainly did.

When Jerry pulled out of our partnership, I was left in financial ruin once again. I was forced to close the chicken processing plant, which could have been the greatest success of my life. We started out processing chicken by hand, and within two years, had amassed so many buyers that a division of Campbell Soup had even shown interest in buying our chicken cordon bleu and chicken Kiev recipes. Sue and I had even gone there with samples, but feeling the pressure of success, I backed out. I retreated to cocaine. By then, I had lost it all; my promise and success were once again devoured by my cocaine addiction, leaving me with nothing.

VI

Facing the Darkness and My Dad

At the time of the close of Gance's Gourmet Foods, I had accumulated a good deal of debt and could see no conceivable way to pay it off. Knowing I had a wife and newborn son to support, I put my pride and anger aside and appealed to the mercy, or perhaps the pity, of my father. I knew what this meant; I had not been able to handle business by myself. No matter how talented or promising I was I still needed my father to come to my rescue. This of course meant once again shouldering the weight of his expectation, or worse, his disappointment –with which I had become familiar by this time in my life. I worked in his kitchen at night, just trying to make ends meet and not even beginning to take on the burden of my debt.

Inside, beneath my frustration at my own failure, I still held on to the dream or maybe even the hope, that I could make something of myself after all. I hoped that I could get out from under my father, make my own way, and find freedom, success, and fulfillment if I just tried. I was a promising restaurateur, after all. Silently and fervently, I held on to this dream, the one that I thought I was realizing with the chicken plant, the dream that was now threatened by my present situation. That dream was alive when I was walking in Owego one day, and happened to notice that a restaurant was for sale downtown, a place I knew as Barry's, though it had changed hands and names since.

My father had always liked the Owego area and had entertained ideas of opening a restaurant there. He had also always liked Barry's. I pushed open the door to the restaurant formerly known as Barry's, and before I had even met Mr. O'Hara, the owner, I was already trying to think of ways to make this my restaurant, a place where I could truly prove that I was not a failure.

"I'm Mike Gance," I introduced myself to Mr. O'Hara, placing emphasis on my last name, hoping to benefit from my father's success and reputation in that regard, "and I see you're selling this place, you know, I remember when this place used to be Barry's, my father..." I trailed off, feeling a little nervous, hoping that Mr. O'Hara would want to do business with me and that he wouldn't sense my fear, or somehow know that I had no money to my name and a terrible addiction that had devoured my past attempts at success.

"Well Mike, I can't imagine letting this place go for less than two-hundred thousand." I bit my lip a little. I hardly had two thousand dollars to my name, let alone two-hundred, taking into account the weight of my debts. But I couldn't let

Mr. O'Hara know that, I had to establish some sort of trust if I was going to make this arrangement work.

"Okay," I said, "I'll work on the financing."

"Well then we'll have to talk more about it." Mr. O'Hara smiled and stretched out his hand to shake mine. I smiled, relieved, while at the same time feeling anxiety mount within me as I wondered how I was ever going to pull it off.

I knew that if I was going to benefit from my father's name and reputation, I would have to stay one step ahead of the game. I worked at night in the restaurant to build up at least a fraction of the money I claimed to have had. By now, I had become used to the habit of being something I was not. I would always hope that the imposter I really was would stay hidden behind whatever façade I was wearing at that particular time. I had played the husband, the inventive businessman, and now the reliable investor. Only I knew how untrue it all was, and it was my plan to keep it that way.

Exposure can be a funny thing. On one hand, it can bring a sense of relief, and a real chance to make things right. I had experienced this once before, the first time my drug problem had been uncovered, and I was forced to face what I had become. On the other hand, exposure can also bring even more shame and turn someone away from the very authenticity that can set them free. Shame is rarely an effective motivator for real growth and healing, but rather, it sets the stage for anger, resentment, and bitterness. All three of these things began to brew inside of me when I received a phone call from Mr. O'Hara.

"Deal's off Mike." O'Hara's voice was flat, not so much angry as disappointed. I could hardly even reflect the same sentiment.

"What...how?" I searched for the words, wondering what could possibly have happened when I had worked so hard to hold everything together, to finally get it right.

"Your dad called, told me the truth about you, about the cocaine, Mike. I don't do deals with addicts, can't afford to make an investment that unstable. You gotta understand, Mike, it's just not good business..." He kept talking, but I had stopped listening. When I had hung up the phone, I sat down to take in the fullness of what my father had done. Could he really have doubted me that much? Had I done so little to regain his trust? Was I ever going to be good enough for him? I wondered if perhaps I was good enough, and this was another expression of my father's insecurities and fears. After all, he had been threatened by my success in the past, maybe this was reason enough to sabotage my deal.

For the first time in a long time, I felt as though I was not wholly to blame for my failure. I chose not to confront my father about the situation with the Owego restaurant, admitting to myself that the bank might have found out about my lies anyway, and I would have had to call it off. I continued to work at the restaurant, and on the surface, my relationship with my father went on as though nothing had happened at all. But beneath the surface, my anger was brewing, causing a nearly invisible but very real tension.

I remember the day that this tension finally snapped. I was working in the restaurant and my old friend Phil Pero came to visit me. Phil and I had been friends since grade school and I had seen little of him lately, and I was glad to have the chance to catch up with him. Since it was a busy time of night at the restaurant, I told Phil to go ahead and get a table, I would join him for dinner after things had slowed down. When I finally had the chance to sit down with Phil, he seemed a bit uncomfortable and slowly began to tell me that my father had been talking to him, telling him of all the trouble I had been having over the last few months, of the drugs and the financial troubles, everything. I felt my fists clench as if all my frustrations with my father were becoming too much to handle. I told Phil to come with me.

Phil and I met my father in the lobby of the restaurant; I sat down on the couch facing Phil with my father next to me. I was seething.

"I haven't seen Phil in six months, and now he comes in and you go ahead and tell him all kinds of stuff! If you have so many problems with me, why don't you tell me?" I was finished hearing about how badly I had messed up, I was sick of my father not protecting me, because I knew deep inside that families should protect, they should love; they should do so much of what my father did not do and had never done. My father looked at me, maybe a little shocked that I had spoken to him like that. He said something that would change my life forever.

"Take your wife, take your kid, and get out!" My father's suggestion only reminded me that I was living on his good graces, rent-free in the apartment house that I was unable to finish. But at that point, I was angry enough not to care. I just knew that I had to speak my part, release the anger that had been building up since the issue with the Owego restaurant.

That night, I walked into the apartment house and closed the door behind me. I knew I needed to tell Sue what had happened, although part of me wanted to do no such thing. I wanted to protect her, and to continue living as though I had it all together. But this time I knew that I had no chance of getting away with it. I had nothing left.

"My father...he kicked us out." I told her quietly. Sue's eyes grew wide.

"What, how? How could he do that? What...what will happen now?" Her voice was pleading. Mine wasn't, it was defeated as I answered her,

"I don't know." They were honest words.

There was no possible way for me to see it at the time, but my father had done the best possible thing for me by kicking me out and forcing me to stand on my own two feet. For one thing, in taking control of everything, my father had assumed my debt from the chicken plant, and he consolidated the loans in order to pay them off. It was as though I had a clean slate, a chance to start over on my own.

I had more than that, even though I did not know it. For the first time in my life I was free of my father's control, his pressures and expectations. I did not have to answer to him. I still had my personal problems, my insecurities, my fears, and of course, my addiction. But my addiction, as I often said to myself, was a way to cope with the pressures of my life, mostly those put on me by my inability to deal with the stress. So much of that stress had been put on me by my father, and now, free from his control, I found myself able to manage my addiction, as I always could in a time of crisis.

As I went the next few days without a job, I thought about the present state of my life. Up until that point, I had not really known myself apart from working for my father, as I had done since I was ten years old. I had never been without a job to do, without something demanding my time and efforts. Now, without my father on my back and a job to go to each night, I felt a strange sense of freedom, and I even began to see a vision of a life without cocaine, a life that could be mine, I thought, now that I was no longer subject to my father's control. If cocaine had been the bandage on a wound in my life, perhaps this time could be one of healing, and my long-time coping habit could become obsolete. I hoped it to be true, as I wanted to be free from cocaine just as much as I wanted to be free from my father's control.

I was wrong. The wound inside of me, the one that I had attempted to bandage up with cocaine, money, and work was not from my father. The feelings of rejection and betrayal I felt from my father were only a symptom of the real brokenness of my heart, and his acceptance and love were not the cure. I had yet to discover the real depth of my pain, the real sickness that had been infecting me for years. The real need in my heart was for far more than a father, it was for a Savior, a way for the guilt and shame of my life to be washed away, not just covered up.

Although my father had hurt me deeply, I could not place all the blame for what I had become on his shoulders. My failures and shortcomings were my own. In the end, I needed to be rescued, saved, from none other than myself. But as is far too often the case in situations such as these, it was only with more time and more loss that I would finally see the hard truth.

VII

Failing One Last Time

Late in the summer of 1985, after my father had ended his association with me, I met a man named Jim Rotella. He was dating a girl who Sue and I knew from our old apartment house, and the four of us went to Spiedie Fest together. I learned that Jim was trying to sell Oliver's, restaurant right in the heart of Binghamton.

My attention was piqued as I remembered the Owego deal I had wanted so much, the one that my father had sabotaged. After the disaster with Gance's Gourmet Foods and the falling out of the Owego restaurant, I had all but abandoned my hope of seeing one of my ventures in the food business succeed. In that moment, something inside of me told me that I should investigate this offer and that perhaps I was being given a second, or rather a third, chance at my original dream. There was also a part of me – a prideful part – that secretly relished the idea of being in competition with my father's restaurant in Endicott. I wanted to show him that I could be a success and that I could do so without a dime of his money.

I made Jim Rotella an offer. I had to be careful in my choice of banks for the financing. I had gone through the Owego National Bank when I was trying to buy O'Hara's a few months earlier, and since that deal had fallen through so terribly, I did not think it likely that they would be willing to take a chance on me. The Binghamton Savings Bank had no idea of my previous shenanigans, but that was not the only problem I faced. I knew that I had no collateral to put up for the loan. Nevertheless, I refused to accept defeat, not when I had the chance to prove myself and to land on my feet at last.

I told the Binghamton Savings Bank that I had recently purchased Oliver's and wanted to take out a loan to remodel it. The truth was, I had not bought anything yet, but I needed to establish some sort of collateral if I was going to take out a loan. The bank believed me and lent me $36,000. Meanwhile, I had set up a private agreement with Jim Rotella to give him $20,000 of that money as a down payment and I would use the remaining $16,000 to actually remodel and open the restaurant. It was a risky thing to do, as I really left myself with very little to get started. Sue had done some decorating in the past and had offered to help me get the place ready for business.

During the next six weeks, Sue and I worked night and day to redecorate Oliver's. Despite the stress, it was a very good time for our marriage. Up until this point we really hadn't spent time learning how to be married. Our relationship had endured crisis after crisis with little time to be together the way we were before we had been married. Not only were we spending time together, but we were also working together, making a longtime dream of mine come true. In years before, I had worked long hours at the restaurant apart from Sue, and even when I came home was still separated from her by cocaine addiction, which I was always hiding from her. But now things were different.

As was my habit during times of real necessity, I was able to keep my addiction at bay, more for lack of funds than anything else. Not only that, but I was also not dealing with my father for the first time in my life. He wasn't looking over my shoulder, our shoulders, waiting for me to mess up again. I felt free.

That was why starting the restaurant on my own, independent from my father, was good for me in many ways. Despite my talent and promise in the restaurant business, I had always dealt with my share of insecurities, mostly due to his critical eye. But now, I was accomplishing something without his help or criticism. Now that I was free from working under my father, I had a chance to really work with my wife. I was beginning to truly appreciate the person she was and the team that we made together.

Looking back, I can undoubtedly see God's favor towards us in those challenging times. We got by everyday with just enough, which sometimes meant selling chairs we weren't using at the restaurant just to have enough money to buy groceries. But Sue and I would not recognize the hand of God for quite some time. We were just at a point in our lives where there was no cocaine, alcohol, or lies. It was a time when we were beginning to search for answers, but we had discovered no real ones yet. Nevertheless, God's provision and protection covered us, even though we were unaware.

I named the restaurant M.A. Gance's, after myself, taking advantage of the good reputation that went along with the Gance name. This of course enraged my father who knew, as well as I, that my Binghamton restaurant would attract some of his own clientele and that I was riding on his success. In truth, I was not. One man had come to work for me from Gance's in Endicott. Other than him, I hired all of my own personnel and cooked all of the food myself. It was my restaurant where I could use all the ideas that my father had feared. I was free to make my own success –and my own failure.

M.A. Gance's was an amazing success. Until then, there had not been a restaurant of that caliber in Binghamton. It seemed as though over night I had gone from having nothing to having it all. But, as always, just when my life began to turn a corner, the darkness of my addiction was waiting, crouching, ready to ruin me, and reminding me that I wasn't good enough to be successful. After a few weeks of being free, while we remodeled the restaurant, I found myself returning to my old habits. Alcohol and cocaine slowly crept back into the comfortable place in my life where they had been so many times before and I did little to resist.

While I was returning to my former self, Sue was turning over a new leaf. I could not deny that something was happening inside of my wife, mostly because she kept talking about a new desire to go to church.

Little did I know Sue's desire was far from new. Before we were married, she had felt a tug on her heart toward God. Years before, when she first left Las Vegas, she remembered praying as the plane was in the air en route to New York. She prayed, asking God to give her a husband, a family, and to get her out of the darkness of Las Vegas that made her feel so dirty inside. In exchange, she would, as she put it, "serve Him the rest of my life." Now things had changed for her and me; the restaurant was successful, Santino was growing, and my drug use was under control, or so she thought. It appeared as though God was making good on His end of the bargain, and Sue wanted to keep her own promise. Not only that, but she was also curious about God, who He was, and if He even kept promises at all.

First Assembly was a growing church in the heart of Binghamton, close to our restaurant. Sue had heard stories about this church and its preacher, Ron Piedmonte. But as is all too common with searching people, Sue did not feel comfortable enough to walk in on any given Sunday and look for answers. A few weeks before opening the restaurant, when we were hiring servers, Sue took note of one applicant in particular named Terri Holly. Terri had put down Pastor Ron Piedmonte as a reference. Although we had filled all of the spots, Sue insisted that we hire Terri. At first I was hesitant, as we could hardly afford to hire more than we needed.

"We do need a hostess, Mike" Sue pointed out. I gave in, and Terri Holly became the first hostess at M.A. Gance's restaurant in Binghamton.

Sue watched Terri Holly, curious if her presence in the restaurant alone would provide her with some of the answers she sought. As Sue watched Terri, Terri was also paying attention to Sue. She was quick to see that something was missing in Sue's life. She knew that Sue was trying to be normal, to raise a child and be a good wife, but all the while struggling to keep everything together with the questions in her heart. Sensing Sue's frustration and pain, she looked for an opportunity to invite Sue to church, unaware not only that Sue had needed that very invitation, but also that Sue's desire had secured Terri's job.

At the same time we hired Terri Holly, we also hired a waiter named Marty. Charming, smooth, and talented, Marty made for a great waiter; he also knew exactly how to organize the other servers and solve any problems we had with seating. We quickly made Marty the head waiter, which we later realized was a terrible mistake. As it turned out, Marty was also addicted to cocaine and chillingly ruthless in supporting his habit.

Marty liked working in the restaurant business because it was a cash business, which made it easier for him to steal money for drugs. My return to alcohol and drugs at that time only served him better, as I was not paying close enough attention to realize that he, as well as I, was dipping into the restaurant's profits in order to support a drug habit. The truth was that even if I had noticed Marty's actions, I might have been reticent to allow investigation of them, knowing I was as guilty as he was.

As is always the case with addictions, it is only a matter of time before they are uncovered. When Marty's addiction came to the surface, he quickly made plans to go to rehab. By this time, I had spent all of our sales tax money on cocaine, which I would eventually have to tell Sue. Once she found that out, I was sure she would leave me like I had expected her to do the first and second time my addiction had cost us so much. In a desperate attempt to convince her that I was still a good guy, I decided to go to rehab with Marty hoping that things could still work out; the vision of life with Sue and without cocaine could still be realized.

By now, I had been addicted to cocaine for years. Thirty days without it did little to cure me. When Sue picked me up at the end of the thirty days, she was told that there was a 90% chance that my addiction would relapse which, of course, it did. Only now, I had regained Sue's trust enough to be able to maintain my addiction in private. Interestingly enough, rehab had worked for me in the sense that I was able to stop drinking. In the past, I had always drunk alcohol whenever I did cocaine. The high of the cocaine was balanced out by the alcohol, and I was able to maintain the appearance of normality. But now, without the alcohol, I had to work harder than before to keep my drug use a secret.

In an effort to convince Sue that rehab had been a success, I began to attend First Assembly with her. By now, she had become quite involved in the church, making friends and finding places to serve. It had become important to her, and if there was any hope of her believing my façade, I knew I had to establish a place for myself there as well. I began going on weekend golfing trips with the pastors at their invitation. I found myself more comfortable in church than I had ever thought possible. After all, my last experience with the church had been a priest breaking my stitches outside of a school dance many years before. I found myself making friends, people who seemed to be good and genuine.

"If only they knew the truth," I would muse to myself as I nursed my cocaine habit in private, "they would never treat me the way they do." It was hardly prideful admittance. I was not now, nor had I ever been proud of my addiction. I knew it was shameful, and I saw how much it had cost me over the years. But I also knew the truth; I couldn't get free, even if I tried. Cocaine always found me. No matter how long I went without it, the old monster of a habit still lived and breathed in me, waiting, never letting go or giving up.

Now with my new identity at church, the chasm between my private life and public performance had grown even larger. I was living a double life, with my problems hidden behind closed doors and my successes on display for all to see. It was a show that had gone on my entire life.

After a while, a double life can begin to take its toll. I began to feel sick inside, I knew that I had to stop using drugs; I could not sit next to my wife on Sunday morning and sing and pray then go home and use cocaine. But somehow, even though I knew it was wrong, I found that I was able to do it, I was able to lead the double life. By now, it was a habit as old and as comfortable as my cocaine ritual and, by now, I had believed it to be a part of who I was. On the outside, I looked as though I had it all together; Sue and I were even involved in several ministries in the church. But inside, I wanted more than anything to feel like a whole person again, not someone divided between a public and private self, yet I did not know how to become who I wanted to be.

I would watch as other people would come into the church, go forward and accept Jesus into their hearts, and have their lives changed. Even though I did accept Jesus as my savior I did not turn my life over to Him. This was the reason why I could not change. Deep inside, I was afraid that it wouldn't work for me, just like rehab, getting married, or even having a son had failed to break me free from my addiction. Nothing had broken through the darkness yet, nothing had been strong enough, and I told myself that this Jesus probably wasn't strong enough either, that I was beyond the grace and forgiveness that I had heard about Sunday after Sunday.

I didn't realize at the time, but I was falling victim to a great and tragic deception. I didn't deny the power or legitimacy of the grace and forgiveness of Jesus, but I did tragically mistake it all for being out of my reach. So week after week, month after month, I would watch others become changed by a gospel that I wanted so desperately to change me, to unite my divided self and make me whole again. But week after week, month after month, I would stay firmly in my seat, telling myself that it just wasn't for me. I just wasn't good enough. I was really just afraid to trust because of the realization that it might actually work.

Looking back, I see how things needed to get worse before they got better. By that time, I was feeling the intense loneliness that accompanies a life of duplicity. Putting up an act is never healthy for the human mind and heart. Besides the truth that God meant for us to live a life of authenticity, there's something deeply unnatural about living a double life and about hiding parts of yourself from those who love you. Duplicity keeps you from being real and, in the end, from being whole. It only made me feel more alone and, in my loneliness, my addiction became worse. This worsening was mostly due to the fact that my addiction became so private. It's one thing to be a drug addict and not care what people around you think, but to live one day to the next with only one mission in mind: to get high. It's another thing completely to have a business, a wife and son, and a serious cocaine addiction that you must keep a secret because your other life, the life you really want, depends on it.

Before long, I began to feel the effects of my double life and the mental toll it was taking on me. Cocaine, which I had thought many years before to be my way out, my escape from the troubles of my own life, turned out to be my prison. I only knew of one way out of this prison: exposure. I began to pray that I would get caught, thinking that perhaps it would propel me into a period of crisis where I would be able to resist cocaine, at least until my life became comfortable enough for me to start using again. Or maybe, if I was caught, God would be able to change me and save me from my addiction like He seemed to do for other people.

As I would stand in that church next to my wife with voices singing all around me, I would pray in all sincerity that my addiction would be discovered, that something dramatic enough would happen to change my life. I prayed this because I knew this was not the life I wanted, nor was it the life I was meant to live. It was in moments like that when I would sit back and wonder how on earth I had gotten to that point.

It seemed like only yesterday that I had started to work in my father's restaurant and I was having a good time going out at night with Mike Tortora. It seemed just yesterday that cocaine was this strange, foreign habit my friends did, but from which I steered clear. "Just yesterday" my attitude toward cocaine was one of disinterest, uncertainty, and even fear. I remember taking that first hit and feeling nothing, wondering what all the excitement was about. As I sat there years later, cocaine – my long held vice and prison – had cost me hundreds of thousands of dollars, had stolen years of my life, and had destroyed so many opportunities as it consumed my life entirely.

As the service would be dismissed and we would leave through the large doors of the church, I wondered if there really could be a way out for me. I would wonder if I would ever be able to just let go of this terrible habit, to let God fix what was wrong with me. I would wonder if I could really be fixed after all.

VIII

The End and the Real Beginning

My prayers were answered. In winter of 1988, Nicky Cruz came to speak at First Assembly. Cruz, a former New York City gang member, now represented Teen Challenge which is a ministry dedicated to helping people become set free and delivered from their addictions and strongholds. Since Sue and I were involved members in the church at this point, guest speakers would often eat at our restaurant. When Nicky Cruz arrived at M.A. Gance's, he was surprised to see that we served alcohol. His surprise had an effect on Sue, who became bothered that we served alcohol in our restaurant while proclaiming ourselves to be Christians and attending church regularly. But that was not the only reason for Sue's concern.

The restaurant had been doing poorly in the last three years. Times were changing; more restaurants were opening around the Binghamton area, dividing our clientele. The late 1980s was also a time of economic recession. These factors all contributed to the restaurant's financial struggles, but they paled in comparison to its greatest challenge which was that I was taking money to support my drug addiction and repeating my old pattern of achieving success only to sabotage it.

Sue, unaware that I was stealing from the restaurant, thought that perhaps our present challenges were God's way of asking us to stop making a profit from alcohol. She approached me about removing our liquor license, believing it to be the best thing we could do for the business. I did not feel at ease with this transition. After all, I knew the real reason for our financial difficulties. Poor Sue, on the other hand, was operating on blind faith and scrambling to remedy what she thought was the real problem.

"Don't you see, Mike?" She said to me when she asked about the liquor license, "Alcohol is a part of our old life, the one we had before we met Jesus. How can we expect God to bless us now when we're still hanging on to the past and not completely trusting in Him?" Sue's argument made sense to me. I also considered that the odds were certainly in her favor since she was a far more genuine Christian than I was at that point. I wanted God to bless us and to break my addiction, so perhaps this move away from liquor was our ticket after all.

"Okay," I agreed, "Let's do it."

Taking out the liquor license did change our lives, but it did not yield the result for which Sue had hoped. While we had much support from the Christian community, it was not enough to carry us when the tough financial waters rose higher. We were forced to close our doors in May, before Mother's Day, three months after removing the liquor license. I remember that I had to roll quarters in order to give Terri Holly her last paycheck. To make matters worse, we still owed Jim Rotella money from buying the restaurant back in 1985. I found myself back where I had been four years earlier: unsure of where to turn and desperate for help. My only comfort was the idea that everyone thought our restaurant was going out of business for honorable reasons. No one knew the role my cocaine addiction had played in our downfall. I found myself in a place of waiting, unsure of what to expect next.

The desire that I had to be exposed sounds crazy, but the truth was that I had had enough. I had been living a double life for such a long time by then and I was just tired. It had taken years, hundreds of thousands of dollars, and so many lies, but I had finally come to the end of myself. So much so that when I closed the doors of the restaurant, my livelihood, my future, I felt a measure of relief. My outer life was in shambles. It was at least starting to reflect my inner life, and the gap between my two worlds was closing. But then again, I had been in this place before. I had been hopeless and lost before; it was all part of the cycle of success and failure, failure and success, that I had been experiencing for as long as I could remember. Of course, I would find something to do that would get us through this difficult time. Of course I would get by without cocaine for a while, the monster of my addiction had always slept in times of crisis, and then, when things started looking up again, I would find a way to sabotage my own success. It was the same cycle and nothing ever changed. I knew that. I knew it more deeply and painfully than I knew anything else. I knew I was beyond help, deliverance, or hope.

I was wrong.

Perhaps it was my hopelessness or maybe my desperate need to be exposed that made me apply for health insurance, that made me consent to a drug test months before. By the time we closed the restaurant, I had forgotten all about the whole thing. That is, until the letter came. Of course it was a rejection letter, one that stated simply that I had tested positive for drug use and was therefore ineligible for coverage. I had expected that. What I had not expected was for Sue to be the first to receive that letter. Ever hopeful, she challenged the insurance company, insisting that I had gone to rehab, that I was, and had been, clean for a while now. It was easy for the insurance company to contest her, sending her a letter with the results of my most recent blood test.

Of all the people who could have been hurt by my double life, Sue stood in the position to be hurt more than anyone. She had been in that position for years now, along with our son, Santino, though he was still too young to really feel the consequences like Sue could. We had been going to church for a few years now, and she thought that I was clean and that I had turned things around. Perhaps it would have been easier for her if I had just been open about my addiction. But as she read that letter, Sue realized that I had done more than maintain my costly addiction at her expense, I had done so while lying to her face and allowing her to believe I had changed. The way that I betrayed Sue through my drug use was terrible but far more devastating was how I lied and how I had raised her hopes only to have them destroyed by that letter. Upon reading it, Sue began to put together the events of the last year, realizing for the first time how it all fit together. She understood why the restaurant had fallen into financial ruin, apart from the business with the liquor license. Like me, she was seeing again how much my addiction had cost those around me, especially her and Santino; and, like me, she too had enough of it all.

Sue called Pastor Piedmonte to tell him what had happened, and to tell him that she was going to leave me. She was finished; finished giving me chances and finished with loving me when I did nothing but bring pain to her life.

Upon receiving the phone call, Pastor Ron Piedmonte called us both into his office. Sitting there, next to Sue and across from Pastor Piedmonte, I figured that this was the end. I deserved to have Sue leave me, to have Pastor Piedmonte tell me I was an awful husband, father, Christian, and any of the other things I had failed to be. Truthfully, I deserved far worse than that.

But that day, in his office, Pastor Piedmonte did the unthinkable. He said something I did not deserve to have him say, not in a thousand years.

"Sue, don't leave your husband," he said, looking into my wife's tear-filled eyes. She wept.

"I don't trust him anymore."

"Don't trust him," Ron Piedmonte said gently, "trust God."

People fail. We are all weak, flawed, and broken. I was certainly no exception. It takes perspective, patience, and unspeakable compassion to extend mercy when it is not due. That day in his office, Ron Piedmonte did just that. In that moment, he chose to see me not as one who had deceived, lied, and stolen, but as one who had sinned and who needed grace. Instead of telling my wife to leave me and turning away in disgust at the depth of my hypocrisy, he urged me to find help. He told me that I should go to Teen Challenge, the ministry that had been the place of deliverance for Nicky Cruz and so many others. I was speechless, and deep inside I knew that it was not what I needed.

"I can't…I just closed the restaurant. Sue and Santino, I can't leave them…" My voice trailed off. On one hand, my addiction was talking, protecting itself, trying to come up with excuses for me to continue in my ways. After all, I had had a wife and son to look after for years but that never stopped me from making terrible choices that had put us all at risk. Yet while the addiction was talking, another voice was gaining strength and becoming clear –the voice of who I really was, the person who wanted out. I prayed for help and God gave me the words. "Michael, you can't go on—" Pastor Piedmonte began, but I cut in.

"No," I said. Pastor Piedmonte looked puzzled, even angry, but he let me go on. "I'm going to stay home, I'm going to read the bible, and I'm going to pray" I said quietly, "and then my life will be different."

"If you're telling the truth," Ron said simply, "then your life will indeed be different. But Michael, if you're lying, then you'll be right back where you started; things will never change."

I knew he was right. If I could just tell the truth for once in my life then maybe, just maybe I could be free. I also knew that underneath my addiction, there was something else to consider; the condition of my very soul. I had tried rehab before, and although Teen Challenge was more than rehab, and I was curious if it could really do me some good, I knew that in the end I needed to stand before God, alone with Him, and answer for what I had done. I believed that if God was going to change me, He could and would do so independent from everyone else. It would just be Him and me.

When I walked out of the office that day, I knew two things at once: I knew that I wanted to be free of cocaine addiction, and I also knew that I was never going to be free from cocaine without the intervention of some power outside of myself. In other words, I knew that I was desperate and unable to make the change on my own. For a drug user, that place of desperation is a crossroads. It is one thing to want help, but a different thing entirely to find exactly what you need to really break free from an addiction.

Although freedom had been my desire, I had done little in my life to realize it. I had been making food for the restaurant for years; I knew what ingredients produced what dishes. Yet in my own life, I had not made the connection that I could not continue to put the same things into it – drugs, desperation, lying, and deception – and hope to generate peace and freedom. But now, in this place of desperation and need, I was beginning to realize this.

My life had blown up, my business was in ruin, and my marriage was on the brink of destruction. As though seeing it all for the first time, I faced my own ugliness, the monster of my addiction, and the devastation that it created, and I did not try to escape. I was finally ready to quit.

Despite the strength of its hold on my life, cocaine was not my biggest problem. All this time, I had been dealing with my addiction, trying to stop it by my own means and through my own power. I had thought cocaine was my biggest enemy, and I could not have been more wrong. Years before cocaine had come into my life the door to it was slowly opening, right from my childhood.

When I first found cocaine, or when it first found me, it crept in because there was a place in my life for it, a place that needed to be filled. Years ago, when I first tried to combat the doubt, desperation, and loneliness in my own heart, cocaine found its place. After a while, I established a pattern, and cocaine became the escape. It was the temporary relief that would make me forget, even for a short while, the depth of my own despair. In all truth, it was not cocaine that needed to be banished from my life; it was the desire for cocaine. Beneath my desire for cocaine was the desire to fill the great emptiness in my heart and life and beneath that was the great emptiness itself. That was the real problem: my insufficiency to do or achieve anything truly good. I had been reminded of this every time I failed. When I felt the sting of failure I numbed it with cocaine, which only made everything worse.

There was nothing I could do anymore. I needed to be rescued from myself, from my sin, and from my fallenness. I did not need rehab, I did not need money, and I did not need success. What I needed, and had needed all along, was a Savior.

I did what I had promised Pastor Piedmonte and Sue that I would do. I stayed home, read my Bible, and prayed. I begged God to help me, at first to fix my addiction, and then to fix me. I knew I needed a miracle, that it would take nothing less to break me of the addiction that had consumed me for so many years. A week into my time of prayer and Bible study, I realized that my desire for cocaine had quietly left me.

I was free.

For once I did what I had said I would do with God, and I did not second guess it. After that meeting with Pastor Piedmonte, I was able to read my Bible and pray in a new way. I expected that when I did what I said I would, God would do something. I wasn't just hoping He would do something, but I knew He would.

As I stayed home reading my Bible, God changed me from the inside out. He took the desire to use drugs out of my life. I can tell you that when you're set free and don't want to use, you're free. I read the Bible and life came into my sick body. I was delivered from the desire to use. The desire that had been so deep in me, and that I could never fight, was gone. I was done with escape and God did it. I didn't have to fight the desire to use anymore because God took it away. He did it.

Looking back, I see that it could not have happened any other way. I needed to lose everything to find the only thing worth having. Sometimes the only way that we grab a hold of God is if we have nothing left in our lives to hold on to. God needed to remove every crutch from my life – my restaurant, my marriage, and my success – until I was left in devastation, all alone, just Michael Gance. I was fully aware of my deep need and I knew that I had gotten to that point by my own actions. There was no one else to blame.

For me that place of brokenness, though certainly not comfortable, was a strange place of peace. It was as though a storm had raged within my life and ripped through until I was left in its calm, finally able to look around and see the damage for what it really was. Only then was I able to stoop to my knees and pick up the pieces of what was left.

IX

Starting Over

I had been delivered from cocaine. Although the addiction was no longer an issue for me, the rest of my life still reflected the damage it had done. Our financial situation was a perfect example of that.

Sue and I decided that it would be a good idea for me to stay out of business for a while. Sue had an opportunity to buy an interior design store in Cortland which was previously owned by a man named Alex Vecchio. It was a good opportunity because Alex had an established clientele and Sue had a talent for design. The issues we had were that the commute from our home to the store in Cortland was one hour each way. It was difficult for us to serve customers properly while also trying to be home on time for our young son Santino. I had taken this time to let someone else lead.

I was so beat up from beating myself up for 10 years of addiction. I had lost all self confidence. I felt that the back seat was a good place for me at the time, but my creative energy kept flowing and before long I starting thinking. I had an idea to start working for the Lord.

I designed and produced bumper stickers for cars that took a stance against drugs. The stickers read "One Nation Under God – Not Drugs." It was a way for me to vocalize my deliverance from drugs. Also, as a way to make extra money, I got a part time job as a salesman for Sweeney's Market a few days a week.

During that time, the hand of God was evident on our lives. He was protecting us and providing for us. The bank through which we had our mortgage went bankrupt which freed us from having to make payments that we could not afford at the time. As a result, we were able to stay in our house on the Vestal Parkway longer than would have been otherwise possible, an entire year in fact.

No matter how wonderfully God provided for us, I was surrounded by reminders of how badly I had messed up. Sue did not trust me and was coming to grips with how much my addiction had cost her and our family.

I felt terrible for Sue, for all I had put her through. She was working at Decors by Alex and trying to dig us out of the financial hole that I had gotten us into. She felt that she had to take on that responsibility and be the primary income producer of the family. I wanted to do something more than just spend a few nights a week working at Sweeny's. So I applied for jobs at restaurants like the Ponderosa, but I was turned down. Since I had been self-employed for most of my life, I had no experience working for other people, and a restaurant did not want to spend time training me only to have me become independent once again.

In the meantime, Sue and I were collecting food stamps. I remember going to the grocery store with our food stamps; it felt as though we had won the lottery. It was a far cry from where I had been not too long before as the owner of a successful restaurant in Binghamton. But, at the same time, this was the best place I had ever been in my life because I was free from cocaine for the first time since my youth.

All too often, people meet Christ and bring a whole host of problems with them. In the moment of salvation, they expect that everything will change quickly and dramatically. On one hand, they are right to think so; Jesus does offer a change in the heart that is radical and incomparable. But on the other hand, the rest of your life does not change in an instant, it takes time. Most of that time is spent relying on God to fully work out the miracle He started. One can easily become discouraged and think nothing will ever change, but that is the moment when you need to trust God the most —when it seems as though everything else is falling apart. I knew that God loved me enough to reach out to me in the midst of my addiction.

In the months and years following, I learned that God's work does not stop at redemption and deliverance, it continues until the fullness of His redemption and deliverance is visible in every area of your life. That process of becoming new can take a long time. It is not an instant change. If it was, there would be no reason to trust God at all, and no reason to stay near to Him. In the end that is what we all need, no matter where or from what we have come.

One evening, I was invited to a meeting for a new multi-level marketing company called Nu Skin by a woman named Mrs. Como. She was a friend of ours who went to another church. Multi-level marketing had grown in popularity during the early 1990s. The idea behind it was that people would buy into a company, sell the products themselves, and then recruit others to sell products and take a small percentage of that profit. The recruits would then find their own workers. The more people you recruit to be a part of your business, the more profit you can potentially generate. I was immediately intrigued with the idea of a business opportunity that could spread so quickly and easily. I wanted to sign up, but I had no credit card and no money to get started. I remember feeling a sense of discouragement when I realized that my former life and choices were once again haunting me and obscuring my future.

When Mrs. Como asked me why I wouldn't buy into the business, I politely told her that I did not have money at that time. In all truth, I had no idea if or when I would ever have that kind of money – let alone a credit card – again. It was then that Mrs. Como handed me her credit card, no questions asked, and told me to get started with it. With my history of lying and cheating, an offering like this was nothing short of a miracle. It was the first of many by which God would show us favor, provision, protection, and grace through the people he placed in our lives.

My involvement with Nu Skin proved to be a profitable endeavor, so much so that we decided to sell the store in Cortland when it became clear that it was not generating enough business. At that point in time, decorating stores were becoming less and less popular. We put the store up for sale, and a local woman showed interest. Soon after we trained her to take it over, she backed out of the deal which left us with no choice but to sue her. We closed the Cortland store soon thereafter. The checks from Nu Skin kept our heads above water during that uncertain time.

Despite my success with Nu Skin, I knew that I really wanted to return to the food business. It had nothing to do with a desire to return to my old life before God's deliverance; I realized that I wanted to take my gifts, talents, and calling and submit them to the same redemptive power that had changed my spirit. God equips us all with gifts. Our sin comes in and distorts the use of our gifts which God intended for good. I was gifted with a good business sense, but because of my sin, I had turned to lying, deception, and stealing because I was under the control of my addiction. Once I was free from that, the natural abilities placed in me by God were free to develop and to be used to glorify Him as He purposed from the beginning. Deliverance is all about the freedom to be what we were meant to be.

I saw my life as a stone sculpture that was covered with a layer of soot, and ruined to the point where one could see the form of what I was made to be, but could not actually see my true substance. God's redemption wiped me clean. He dug beneath the layers of my sin to restore what was underneath: the part of me that was made in His image, the part that was meant to be free all along.

This is true for all of us; God gives us gifts and talents that are meant to be used for His glory and our good, but that plan is derailed when we get caught up in the world. Sin does terrible things to us; it twists things up and changes them for the worse. In redemption and forgiveness is the chance to set things right and restore them to the way they were meant to be.

I knew my re-entry into the food business would be anything but easy. I went to the store one day and bought supplies to make small bag lunches. My thought was that I would make up bag lunches with sandwiches and other goodies and display them in a basket. My sales plan was to build routes in business areas where I could sell to twenty-five or more businesses per route in one day. It was humbling.

After all, I had been the owner of a classy and successful restaurant, but now I was only buying supplies one day at a time because that was how much I could afford. I had no credit so I was literally starting a small business out of my own pocket. Anyone could have told me it was a step down, and they would have been right. But, for the first time in my life, I didn't feel as though I needed to pursue success with everything I had inside me. I just wanted to feed my family. My life belonged to God; my dreams were His, my finances, and even my burdens. My successes were His as well. Suddenly, success had nothing to do with validation and everything to do with bringing honor to God. He was teaching me to work with what I had in my hand, not borrowing, and just living day by day, His way.

As far as my debts went, I knew that God would help me to take care of them in His time. I was thirty-four years old with a terrible reputation, no credit, no college education, and not even a high school diploma. I was doing the one thing I knew how to do: sell food. I had spent years sidetracked by drugs, addiction, and negativity, but now, I was free from all that and free to use my talents with no strings attached.

Soon my lunchtime sales grew popular, and I started other routes. Every morning, the people I had hired to run the routes would come to our home early in the morning to pick up the lunches. They tracked dirt all over Sue's white carpet. Eventually, I had ten routes going at once. Within six months, we grew too large to be operating out of my home kitchen, and we moved into the kitchen my aunts had been using to cook the food for Gance's years before. I only had to pay the cost of utilities.

This was an important time for me because for years no one had trusted me, and with good reason. I was not worthy of anyone's trust, and I had proven that. As I began to slowly ease back into the food business, people started to see that something about me had changed; I was no longer the same person I had been before. Everyone had known how bad I was, they knew my reputation. When my aunts rented me the property to start my own business it was nothing short of a miracle. It can take years for a recovering drug addict to build up the trust that he has lost, but my aunts trusted me even before I had earned it back, and it was their trust that made my new business possible. I was in the food business once again.

This was not only an important time for me as a recovering drug addict, but it was also an important time for me as a Christian. My years of addiction to cocaine had left me feeling as though I was worth nothing and as though I could do nothing well. God places a desire in our hearts to be worth something in this world, to provide for our families, and to make the most of what we have been given. Our sinfulness has warped this God given desire into a lust for success and money when, behind it all, is something valuable and good. Through the sandwich business, God gave me something that my addiction had taken away: my dignity. Just as I was rebuilding things in my life – my marriage, my finances, and my business – God was using this time to rebuild me by changing my priorities, my desires, and my heart.

Financially things were improving. We had been able to stay in the house on the parkway longer than we should have been which worked out well. At the time we had no money for a car. Seeing our need, someone from the church gave us a car, and then Sue's parents gave us the money to buy one of our own. We were living day by day, and hoping to make one dollar become two just to meet our basic needs.

During this time, I had the opportunity to give my testimony at a meeting for Full Gospel which was a Christian organization for business people. They held a dinner at the Sheraton Hotel for which I was the featured speaker. I was able to tell others how God had delivered me from my cocaine addiction and, although things were not perfect, they were a hundred times better than they had been before.

Many people approach deliverance with a fair and understandable amount of skepticism. One of my chief skeptics was, of course, my father. At first, my father certainly did not believe that anything had changed in my heart. After all, he had seen me fail as many times as Sue had, and he had also heard my grandiose promises for change. He had witnessed how so many of my ideas were destroyed by my drug use. He was always hard on me, and this time was no different. His trust was the most difficult to earn back. After months of watching me struggle to make ends meet, working hard at the new business, and staying off drugs, my father eventually came to believe that something was different. He realized that something had to be different if I was managing to keep things together for as long as I had.

As we became more involved at First Assembly of God, we found new friends who came into our lives and helped us make the changes we needed to make. When someone comes to know Christ but the shell of their prior existence is still there, it's important to develop a new circle of friends, both for accountability and fellowship. The outward change must go beyond just adding church to your schedule, but it must spread to transform everything you do. God, in turn, works through new friends to protect and provide for new believers, just as he did for me through Mrs. Como and the Nu Skin business.

My uncle, Jimmy, was one person God used during this time in my life. Despite my tense relationship with my father, I had always gotten along well with his brother.

When I closed the Gance's Gourmet Foods business, Jimmy rented the kitchen and used it as a meat market. Despite his own struggle with alcohol, Uncle Jimmy always showed unconditional love towards me by supporting me no matter what I did. At this time Sue and I would go over to my Uncle Jimmy and Aunt Essie's for dinner many nights and, in our time with them, we grew close to their next door neighbors, John and Patty Farrell, a couple from First Assembly of God. Patty and Sue were in a Bible study together, and soon became good friends. The Farrells had a son Santino's age, and those two boys also became good friends. I still remember summer evenings spent sitting out on the porch with the Farrells and Jimmy and Essie.

One of the terrible prices you pay as a drug addict is that you give up the joy of having a real community. Drug addiction causes you to retreat inside of yourself and to cut off the people who are closest to you because you don't want them to see you for what you really are. It is a protection method. After my drug addiction, I realized that I had been alone for years; even though I worked in a busy restaurant, had a beautiful wife and son, and was constantly interacting with people, it wasn't real. It was not community. I was always hiding and always afraid. The end of my drug addiction was the beginning of many real and honest relationships for me. After years of trying to cope with the hurts in my life and fill the void with cocaine, I realized that I could have what I needed all along.

John Farrell was a prominent business man in Broome County. He was trying to organize an event called Family Days where local businesses would have family picnics for their employees. He intended to take care of the details, such as food. To my surprise, he asked me if I would cater this large event. I was baffled. I had done smaller catering jobs along with my sandwich business for offices and small private parties, but never anything this large where I would have to feed hundreds or maybe even a thousand people.

Despite my initial fear in entering into the deal with John, I worked hard, planned, and in the end, pulled it off. Family Days was a huge success, and after that, John and I were able to get a few more jobs like it. We catered the NYSEG company picnic, and another one for the Raymond Company, which made forklifts. That picnic was not as successful as previous ones. I learned that I had to think farther ahead with catering and anticipate what could go wrong before anything went wrong. I realized that catering was about being conscious of people's feelings and expectations, and that there was more to consider than just food. It was different than running a restaurant in that way. The Raymond job taught me how to think when performing large catering jobs. I learned by doing. I was gaining confidence as a caterer, and found that I really enjoyed doing it as well. I was starting to see miscalculations and setbacks as part of the learning process, not as failure. Before, setbacks would send me quickly towards cocaine which I thought would take away my shame. But as I was gaining catering experience, I had learned to forgive myself and to learn from my mistakes rather than to give in to discouragement and despair.

At this time United Health Services held a very large company picnic every year, and I knew they were looking for it to be catered. Assuming they would be interested in saving money, I put in a bid for the job. I was up against the two biggest caterers in Broome County: E&T Catering and Banquet Masters. There was no reason for United Health Services to pick me, who was inexperienced and young, to do their picnic. When they saw how I could save them quite a bit of money, United Health Services hired me for the job.

4,500 people came out to the picnic that year, and they were so pleased that they made sure to ask me to do the picnic the following year as well. When one job ended God would provide us with another one.

I was learning how to be a caterer, husband, father, and Christ-follower during this time. I was also learning about God's assurance and provision. When you look out in front of you, you can only see so far to the horizon. God never promised to line that distance with the specifics of how and when He would provide for all of our needs. Oftentimes, God provides what is needed when it is needed. Perhaps that is why when Jesus taught us to pray, He told us to ask God for "daily bread", just enough for today. This way, we would remember to come back and ask again the next day, and the day after that. If God gave us all of the answers and all that we need in advance, we would distance ourselves from Him, imagining ourselves to be self-sufficient. God wants us to stay near to, trust in, and depend on Him. God was teaching me to live my life from one day to the next; I was dependent on His favor and provision, leaning not on myself, and never straying too far from Him. This is what He wants from all of us, and certainly, this is all that we need.

In 1992, Sue and I bought a town house. I had been working very hard and we had saved up about ten thousand dollars. My father, moved by the changes I had made in my life over the last two years, put that town house in his name and gave Sue and me the mortgage. This was a momentous event in my relationship with my father. After years of distrusting me and of watching and waiting for me to fail, my father trusted me enough to sign his name to my house. He finally believed in me enough to support me.

I want to make one thing perfectly clear. You can try all you want to make people believe in you and build up what you once had, but God is the only one who brings restoration. He's the only one who can actually change someone's mind about you and clean the slate so they can see you anew. My relationship with my father was complex, and so much of who I was seemed to be wrapped up in it. As I came to realize the importance of father-son relationships, it made me want to pursue a deeper relationship with Santino which I was finally able to do after years of being so absent and involved only in my drug use. It seemed that God was always finding new areas of my life to revive and restore.

God's restoration was evident in so many things, but particularly in the area of my physical health. My finances, business, and marriage were not the only things negatively affected by my cocaine use; my body had begun to bear the terrible signs of an addict. I had been using cocaine for seven years by the first time I went to a doctor about my headaches. It was around the time I had the restaurant in Binghamton. The doctor took one look inside my nose, and begged me to cease my cocaine use.

"You've been blowing your nose a lot, I take it," he said. I nodded, although the words "a lot" were a gross understatement when it came to how often I blew my nose. The doctor shook his head.

"You think you're just blowing your nose, but that stuff that's coming out, that is bone and cartilage, Mr. Gance. You've destroyed the inside of your nasal passages, you simply must..."

He spoke, but I was hardly in a place to listen.

Years later, after I was delivered from cocaine, I accepted the daily headaches as a residual consequence of my prior life. I prayed that God would give me the grace to accept it. Then one day, I realized that I had stopped blowing my nose.

My headaches had also ceased. That was it, my nose just healed as though nothing had happened in the first place.

Now, looking back on that, I laugh to myself. That is so very much what God does; He restores even the worst of cases. He heals when we don't deserve it, and brings us back to how we were meant to be: whole.

God had many ways of teaching Sue and I how to live, and some of those lessons were more difficult than others. By this time, I had learned the importance of taking responsibility for my choices, even the ones I had made under the influence of drugs. It became evident that we owed the state over $225,000 in sales tax, and owed the IRS over $60,000 because of years of mismanagement at the restaurant and the use of the money for other things. It was enough to make anyone want to run away, but we did not. We stayed and dealt with the problems head on, and trusted God to give us the strength and wisdom to do so. In the end, both the IRS and the state settled with me on the debt for less than 20% of what we owed which was another miracle that showed us God's faithfulness. God was not only giving us a future, He was also helping us repair the damages of the past so that we would not have to be afraid of it anymore.

Looking back I see that such a miracle would not have been possible if I had tried to run from my problems, or tried to cheat my way through as I had done in the past. In choosing obedience, we choose God's protection and provision. Choosing obedience also meant following God even when things didn't make sense or when we could not see the way out – as was evident with the tax situation. As Sue and I learned how to obey and listen for the voice of God amidst other voices, we also learned to trust in the midst of change and confusion, which was a discipline that would be put to the test sooner than we could have foreseen.

Up until that point, our faith in God had been growing and we owed so much of that to our involvement at First Assembly of God and to the community we had found there. In 1997, that community faced a serious challenge. Pastor Piedmonte announced his retirement from the church, and some of our church's congregants were not happy with the selection process of the new pastor. A lot of people were very upset when one of the staff pastors was not selected as Pastor Piedmonte's replacement. This discontent became a major source of conflict in the church, which had been an important place of growth and safety for us for years now. A whole host of families left the church at once, gutting it of its many faithful congregants. Among them were many families with which we had been especially close.

It was terrible to see how a church could be so deeply and adversely affected by a human conflict. For new believers, like me and Sue, such a crisis could have been the breaking point of our faith. It was a chance for us to examine what we had come to believe so fervently. Had we really placed our confidence in God or in the church family made up of people just as damaged and fallen as we were? That question, the question of loyalty, or placed faith, is the one that is asked of all Christians in the face of crisis. It is in crisis that truth is revealed, just as in the parable Jesus told of two men who weathered the same storm:

> *"...everyone who hears these words of mine and puts them into practice is like a wise man who built his house on the rock. The rain came down, the streams rose, and the winds blew and beat against that house; yet it did not fall, because it had its foundation on the rock. But everyone who hears these words of mine and does not put them into*

*practice is like a foolish man who built his house on
sand. The rain came down, the streams rose, and
the winds blew and beat against that house, and it
fell with a great crash." (Matthew 7:24-27, NIV)*

The man who built his house on the rock was able to
withstand the external forces that threatened him, while the
man who had built his house on the sand had no foundation,
nothing to hold his house together through the storm. It can
be hard to build a house on the rock by disciplining yourself
to lean on the promises of God rather than taking the reins in
your own life. It can be harder still to continue to trust God
in the midst of a storm when everything inside of you wants
to quit, walk away, and give up.

With our church family falling apart, and our financial
situation still precarious, Sue and I could have walked away.
At that point, however, I knew that I had nowhere else to go.
I had lived for years on my own power, in my own way, and it
had led to nothing but despair and disaster. I knew there was
nothing out there for me apart from the future that God had
in store for me, and I kept that in mind as Sue and I continued
to pray, read our Bibles, and attend and serve at church, all
the while hoping that the difficult time would pass. We didn't
know when things would improve, but we knew that when
they did, we wanted to be found faithful and having never lost
hope in God, whom I had come to trust more than anyone,
even myself.

We stayed, and day by day, God worked in our lives,
chipping a little bit more of the old Mike and Sue away and
making us into the people we were meant to be all along.
Meanwhile, as God remained the same, life around us began
to change. The church recovered slowly from its conflict, and

our catering business built up a greater clientele and grew larger.

One great moment in particular for the business came in the early 1990s when I was doing catering for some rock bands. I had made connections through my friend Stu Green who had been booking the bands himself. I also had a few old connections from years before I started using cocaine. During the summer of 1992, Sue, Santino, and I went to a Christian music festival called Kingdom Bound. In and of itself, Kingdom Bound is a miracle that has a great story behind it. Freddie Casserta, a rock and roll promoter, had started the festival a few years back after he had given his life to the Lord, and wanted to channel his talents to organize a festival that would bring families together for entertainment and growth. Sue, Santino, and I had such a wonderful time there and I took note of the many performing artists and wondered who was doing the catering. I called Freddie Casserta to make a bid for the job. He told me that the same caterer had been doing their festival for years, but that he would keep me in mind if they ever needed me for the future and asked me to send a business card. Freddie had a reputation for being quite disorganized with paper work and though I sent him a card, I didn't expect him to keep it and remember to call me.

Five years later in 1997, I was surprised to receive a call from Freddie telling me that their caterer was not going to be able to do the festival that year, and asking me if I was interested in taking over. Kingdom Bound became one of our best jobs, and we have kept them as clients for many years, even to this day. Looking back I see how God, even in this situation, was teaching us to remain faithful and to trust him with our futures. Freddie did not offer me the job when I asked for it, and he did not offer it the following year, or the year after that. Freddie called me five years later when I thought I would never hear from him.

Sometimes serving God is like that; you don't always get what you want when you want it. Things don't happen in your time and in your way. In uncertainty, God teaches you to trust in His provision. In pain and suffering, God teaches you to trust His goodness. In times of waiting, God teaches you to trust His timing. God's plan is to provide for us and to bless us, but it is also to grow, change, and heal us in the meantime. In teaching us to wait and trust, God does more than give us what we need; He shapes us into who He desires us to be.

I had learned to be patient as God worked a miracle in my life and I then had to learn that God's miracles outside of my life often take time as well. All too often, when people come to know the redeeming power of Jesus and the forgiveness of God, they come excited about God's promises of care and provision. But when the world around them does not change, or when disaster comes, they give up and perhaps call it a lie. There is no greater tragedy than the person who refuses to wait on and trust in God. Jesus said "I am the vine; you are the branches. If a man remains in me and I remain in him, he will bear much fruit." (John 15:5, NIV)

The years passed, my catering business grew, and soon, times of financial uncertainty became just a memory for me and Sue. We continued our involvement at First Assembly. I became a trustee after being elected to the church board. By this time it had been thirteen years since my deliverance from cocaine addiction. Having financial experience from my years of being self-employed, I began to work with the church treasurer as his assistant for what turned out to be his last year in that position. When a job transfer made him unable to continue serving the church, he stepped down, and the pastor of the church at this time, Bill Kirk, asked me to take his place as church treasurer.

I, who years before had stolen money for drugs, lied to get bank loans, had been deceitful, selfish, and dishonest, was being asked to handle the church's finances. When I look back on that moment, I can see that God's redemption of my life had come full circle. When I was broken inside and a slave to my selfish addictions, God did more than rescue me –He forgave me. He could have stopped there, but in His love, He did not and still does not stop at simply showing us mercy by sparing us what we truly deserve. He gives us what we don't deserve: grace. In His grace, He restores. God doesn't just stop us from being destroyed, He builds us up. Where rescue, forgiveness, mercy, and grace would be enough, God restores. He restores life where there was death, He restores hope where there was despair and, in my case, He restored honor where there was none.

He brought me from my position as a lying drug addict to being the treasurer of a large church. All I had to do was give Him control of my life and stop holding on to the things that I thought could offer me answers. Looking back, it was anything but a fair trade. That is what redemption is all about, God giving us a clean slate in exchange for our sin. Who could resist a trade like that?

From the start of our lives, we are made to be completely dependent on God. God gives us our lives, preserves them with His grace and provision, and makes us a part of His master plan. It is when we venture outside of where we're supposed to go and what we are meant to be, that we find ourselves in bondage, just as I was. When I had spent time in rehab, I discovered that other members of my family; aunts, uncles, and cousins, had also had their own problems with drugs. Our tendency toward rebellion is sewn into the fabric of our humanity, as is our need for a Savior. Certainly everyone stumbles into bondage in his or her own way, and it is always costly. But the good news for me, and for everyone else, is that Jesus came to break the chains of bondage, to give life, and to give it more abundantly. He came to call us back into God's plan and purpose no matter how far we've wandered away. God promises to provide for all of our needs in the process. The only thing we need to do is come to Him, no matter how broken we are.

Mine is a story of a second chance. It is the story of a man whose life was heading in one direction and who was trying to fill the longing in his heart with everything but the one thing it was meant to hold. It is the story of a man who deserved punishment and death, but was given back his life and more by a God who never stopped reaching out, even when that man turned away from Him. It is the story of how God's love is stronger than our sin, and deeper than even our deepest darkness. It is the story of how I was rescued, forgiven, and restored. It is my story, and it can be yours too when you stop running and stop trying to fix it your way. Instead allow God to intervene in the chaos of your life and bring the only peace and joy that is real, true, and eternal. Give God a chance today!

About the Author

Michael Gance lives in Upstate New York with his wife Suzann. He has a son, Santino and a daughter-in-law Erin. He is an accomplished business man and also serves as the Treasurer for First Assembly of God, where he was saved in 1986. Mike's greatest hope is that those who are struggling would come to realize that Jesus is the answer and He can set anyone free from anything, lives can be changed, and hope can be restored.

To Contact:
michaelgance@gmail.com